A Feast of Poetry

A Feast of Poetry

Compiled by John Smith

Decorations by Winifred Boon

Burke Publishing Company Limited
LONDON ★ TORONTO ★ NEW YORK

First published 1988
Introduction and editing of this anthology
© John Smith 1988
Illustrations © Burke Publishing Company Limited 1988

Publishers' Note

Although every effort has been made to obtain copyright permissions, it has not always been possible to trace the copyright-owners. Those few whose names are not included in the *Acknowledgements* are invited to apply to the Publishers.

Drama teachers and others wishing to obtain permission to give public recitals of any of the poems contained in the anthology are requested to apply direct to the copyright-owners listed in the *Acknowledgements*.

CIP data
A Feast of poetry.
  1. English poetry
  I. Smith, John, 1924 –
  821'.008   PR1175
ISBN 0 222 01063 0 Hardbound
ISBN 0 222 01075 4 Paperback

Burke Publishing Company Limited
Pegasus House, 116-120 Golden Lane, London EC1Y 0TL, England.
Burke Publishing (Canada) Limited
Registered Office:
20 Queen Street West, Suite 3000, Box 30, Toronto, Canada M5H 1V5.
Burke Publishing Company Inc
Registered Office:
333 State Street, PO Box 1740, Bridgeport, Connecticut 06601, USA
Printed in England by Purnell Book Production Limited

Acknowledgements

Thanks are due to the following poets, agents and publishers for permission to reprint certain poems in this anthology:

Dannie Abse for *Hunt the thimble*

The Oxford University Press Ltd. for the *The Window* by Conrad Aiken, reprinted from *Collected Poems, Second Edition*

Constable Publishers, W.W. Norton & Co. Inc. and A.P. Watt Ltd. for *Written for his lost Nightingale* by Alcuin, reprinted from *Medieval Latin Lyrics,* translated by Helen Waddell

Samizdat Publishers for *Autumn Crocuses* by Guillaume Apollinaire, translated by Oliver Bernard

Faber & Faber and Random House Inc. for *Honey Harvest* by Martin Armstrong

A.D. Peters & Co. Ltd. for *Carry her over the water* and *On this Island* by W.H. Auden, reprinted from *Collected Poems*

John Murray (Publishers) Ltd. for *Agricultural Caress* by John Betjeman, reprinted from *Collected Poems*

The Modern Poetry Association for *Rachel at Kittyhawk* by Edward Brash, reprinted from *Poetry*

Jonathan Graham Burton for *Scratch*

Alan Ayling (translator) for *Leaf By Leaf* by Liu K'O Chuang

Collins Education and Granada Publishing Ltd. for *Nobody loses all the time* by e e cummings, reprinted from *Complete Poems 1913-1962*

David Higham Associates Ltd. and Macmillan Publishing Co. Ltd. for *Ballad of the Bread Man* by Charles Causley, reprinted from *Collected Poems*

Michael Hamburger for *Death Fugue* by Paul Celan

Michael Connors for *Song, for my Cat Suki*

Hamish Hamilton Ltd. for *Chez M. Prieur* by Paul Dehn, reprinted from *The Day's Alarm*

Chatto & Windus, the Hogarth Press for *Lament for the Great Yachts* by Patric Dickinson

Sidgwick & Jackson Ltd. for *Moonlit Apples* by John Drinkwater

Chatto & Windus, The Hogarth Press and The Oxford University Press for *The Groundhog* by Richard Eberhart, reprinted from *Collected Poems 1930-1976*

Faber & Faber Ltd. and Harcourt Brace Jovanovich, Inc. for *Cousin Nancy* by T.S. Eliot, reprinted from *Collected Poems 1909-1962*

The Executors of the Estate of Robert Graves and A.P. Watt Ltd. for *The Door* and *The Legs* by Robert Graves, reprinted from *Collected Poems 1975*

ACKNOWLEDGEMENTS

The Oxford University Press for *Walking Song* by Ivor Gurney, reprinted
  from *Collected Poems of Ivor Gurney*, edited by P.J. Kavanagh
Phoebe Hesketh for *Walking on Air*
Taner Baybars (translator) for *'Welcome, My Woman!'* by Nazim Hikmet
Philip Hobsbaum for *This Small Hostility*
Jonathan Cape Ltd., Holt, Rinehart & Winston Publishers and The Society
  of Authors for *On Wenlock Edge* and *When I was One-and-Twenty* by
  A.E. Housman, reprinted from *Collected Poems*
Faber & Faber and Harper & Row Publishers Inc. for *View of a Pig* by
  Ted Hughes, reprinted from *Lupercal*
Routledge & Kegan Paul PLC for *A Hope for those Separated by War* by
  Sidney Keyes, reprinted from *Collected Poems*
The Oxford University Press for *In Defence of Drunkards* by
  Jan Kochanowski, reprinted from *Five Centuries of Polish Poetry 1450-1970*
Alan Ayling for *Since I Left* by P'u-Ch'ing P'ing Le
A.D. Peters & Co. Ltd. for *Field of Autumn* and *Day of these Days* by
  Laurie Lee, reprinted from *Selected Poems*
John Johnson Ltd. for *Stars* by Peter Levi
Macmillan Publishing Co. for *Yet Gentle with the Griffin Be* by Vachel Lindsay
George MacBeth for *The Red Herring*
The Literary Trustees of Walter de la Mare and The Society of Authors for
  Farewell and *The Rainbow* by Walter de la Mare
Samuel Menashe for *Sudden Shadow, A Pot poured out* and *Salt and Pepper*
The Ohio Press and The Swallow Press for *Cossante* by Pero Meogo,
  translated by Yvor Winters
Carcanet New Press for *At Porthcothan* by Christopher Middleton, reprinted
  from *111 Poems*
Eyre & Spottiswoode Ltd. (The Associated Book Publishers) for *Sensitive,
  Seldom and Sad* and *It Makes a Change* by Mervyn Peake
Faber & Faber and New Directions Publishing Corporation for *Ancient Music*
  by Ezra Pound, reprinted from *Personae*
Punch for two poems
Laurence Pollinger Ltd. and Random House Inc., by permission of Alfred A.
  Knopf Inc., for *Lady Lost* by John Crowe Ransom, reprinted
  from *Selected Poems, 3rd Edition, Revised and Enlarged*
David Higham Associates Ltd. and Methuen & Co. for *Pastures* and *Epitaph*
  by Sir Herbert Read, reprinted from *Collected Poems*
Johnathan Cape Ltd. for *Lives* by Henry Reed, reprinted from *A Map of
  Verona*
Methuen, London for *The Lesser Lynx* by E.V. Rieu, reprinted from *The
  Flattered Flying Fish*
Jeremy Robson for *Song for a Season*
Robson Books Ltd. for *Song for a Season* and *Moods of Rain* by
  Vernon Scannell
Hardiman Scott for *To Heaven by Bus*
John Smith for *The Stirring, Day* and *Feet*
James MacGibbon and New Directions Publishing Co. for *Jumbo* and *The
  Passing Cloud* by Stevie Smith
Faber & Faber and Random House Inc. for *Ultima Ratio Regum* by
  Stephen Spender, reprinted from *Selected Poems*

ACKNOWLEDGEMENTS

Macmillan & Co. and The Society of Authors for *A Glass of Beer* by James Stephens, reprinted from *Collected Poems*

Faber & Faber and Random House Inc., by permission of Alfred A. Knopf Inc., for *Disillusion at Ten o'Clock* by Wallace Stevens, reprinted from *The Collected Poems of Wallace Stevens*

J.M. Dent & Sons Ltd. for *Wet through* by Hal Summers

Dodd, Mead & Co. Inc. and William Heinemann Ltd. for *Summer in Spring* by Arthur Symons, reprinted from *Collected Poems*

J.M. Dent & Sons Ltd. and David Higham Associates Ltd. for *Poem in October* by Dylan Thomas, reprinted from *Collected Poems*

New Directions Publishing Corporation and Laurence Pollinger Ltd. for *Suzanne* by William Carlos Williams, reprinted from *Collected Later Poems*

Peter Yates for *The Window*, reprinted from *Petal and Thorn*

Macmillan Publishing Co. and A.P. Watt Ltd. for *Down by the Salley Gardens* and *The Second Coming* by W.B. Yeats, reprinted from *The Collected Poems of W.B. Yeats*

John Johnson Ltd. for *Schoolmaster* and *Babiy Yar* by Yevgeny Yevtushenko © Robin Milner-Gulland and Peter Levi 1962

Contents

Conversation between Courses

The Main Course

CONTENTS

x

Conversation between Courses

Afters

CONTENTS

Introduction

A Feast of Poetry has been compiled in response to the many requests from readers of my previous anthologies *The Pattern of Poetry, My Kind of Verse,* and *My Kind of Rhymes.* As in those earlier collections my main aim has been to proffer a wide-ranging miscellany which, while primarily aimed at young readers, will, I hope, give pleasure to people of maturer years.

Poetry is indeed a feast for the mind but, sadly, it can often seem to the newcomer very stodgy and unappetising fare; a "subject" to be studied rather than an "art" to be enjoyed. Of course the greatest poetry will often shock us into a new awareness of ourselves and the world in which we live; offer insights into the world of the Spirit, stimulate our intellect and affect our emotions. But there are also less exalted works which move us in a subtle way by an innocent charm, or by their jaunty rhythms or audacious word-play.

In these pages I have tried to assemble an anthology of poems and verses as appealing and balanced as a well-planned banquet. Perhaps a few eyebrows may be raised at the inclusion of certain frivolities, or poems whose "sentimental" air may seem strange in these all too violent times, but if a delicate soufflé is no substitute for good roast beef, it is not the less desirable at the right time and in the right place.

So I hope that masterpieces by such geniuses as Keats or Marvell, Hopkins or Yeats will be complemented by the children's poems, entertainments and minor delights which surround them.

Notwithstanding the headings of the various sections, it is not to be thought that because a poem is included in "Starters" or "Afters" it is necessarily of less importance than those included in "The Main Course". It is a question of "tone" rather than substance that has dictated its positioning.

It only remains for me to add that none of the poems in this anthology appear in any of the collections mentioned above, and to hope that, like those, it will be given a welcome by lovers of poetry and verse in all its many and varied forms.

JOHN SMITH

Starters

The Window : *Conrad Aiken*

She looks out in the blue morning
and sees a whole wonderful world
she looks out in the morning
and sees a whole world

she leans out of the window
and this is what she sees
a wet rose singing to the sun
with a chorus of red bees

she leans out of the window
and laughs for the window is high
she is in it like a bird on a perch
and they scoop the blue sky

she and the window scooping
the morning as if it were air
scooping a green wave of leaves
above a stone stair

and an urn hung with leaden garlands
and girls holding hands in a ring
and raindrops on an iron railing
shining like a harp string

an old man draws with his ferule
in wet sand a map of Spain
the marble soldier on his pedestal
draws a stiff diagram of pain

but the walls around her tremble
with the speed of the earth the floor
curves to the terrestrial centre
and behind her the door

opens darkly down to the beginning
far down to the first simple cry
and the animal waking in water
and the opening of the eye

she looks out in the blue morning
and sees a whole wonderful world
she looks out in the morning
and sees a whole world.

Starters

Will there really be a morning? : *Emily Dickinson*

Will there really be a morning?
Is there such a thing as day?
Could I see it from the mountains
If I were as tall as they?

Green : *D. H. Lawrence*

The dawn was apple-green,
    The sky was green wine held up in the sun
The moon was a golden petal between.

She opened her eyes, and green
    They shone, clear like flowers undone
For the first time, now for the first time seen.

Inversnaid : *Gerard Manley Hopkins*

This darksome burn, horseback brown,
His rollrock highroad roaring down,
In coop and in comb the fleece of his foam
Flutes and low to the lake falls home.

A windpuff-bonnet of fáwn-froth
Turns and twindles over the broth
Of a pool so pitchblack, féll-frówning
It rounds and rounds Despair to drowning.

Degged with dew, dappled with dew
Are the groins of the braes that the brook treads through,
Wiry heathpacks, flitches of fern,
And the beadbonny ash that sits over the burn.

What would the world be, once bereft
Of wet and wildness? Let them be left,
O let them be left, wildness and wet;
Long live the weeds and the wilderness yet.

Wet through : *Hal Summers*

Being now completely wet through to the skin
I begin to see I was a fool to mind it.
This that wets me, what is it but good rain
That has left half England growing greener behind it?

The trees are drunk with it; the greedy grasses
Hold up their infinitesimal hands to catch it;
The pools to hold it break their looking-glasses
And the ditch runs with a stormy noise to match it.

This cloud like a tanker or rich merchantman
Has come from far, with the great wind that fans it,
And over Exmoor or Cotswold it began
To unload its precious freight, after a long transit.

Then eastward over the shires it took its hour
By Avon and by Thames, by Test and Kennet,
By Arun and by Ouse, Medway and Stour,
Pouring such wealth, the earth cannot contain it.

And now like medieval pilgrims or
Sturdy Elizabethan beggars I,
Wet to the skin, look up, and see the core
Of darkness rent in golden rags on high.

The last drops fall; the riddled pools resume
Their smooth reflections; only the hidden freshet
Is loud still, running its tunnelled gloom
Where strawberry, sloe, and bramble shoots enmesh it.

Outpacing me, the enormous cloud stems on,
Its hold still heavy-laden, its hull black,
And leaves a world new-minted; even the sun
Seems washed, and with adored heat burns my back.

Moods of Rain : *Vernon Scannell*

It can be so tedious, a bore
Telling a long dull story you have heard before
So often it is meaningless;
Yet, in another mood,
It comes swashbuckling, swishing a million foils,

Feinting at daffodils, peppering tin pails,
Pelting so fast on roof, umbrella, hood,
You hear long silk being torn;
Refurbishes old toys, and oils
Slick surfaces that gleam as if unworn.
Sometimes a cordial summer rain will fall
And string on railings delicate small bells;
Soundless as seeds on soil
Make green ghosts rise.
It can be fierce, hissing like blazing thorns,
Or side-drums hammering at night-filled eyes
Until you wake and hear a long grief boil
And, overflowing, sluice
The lost raft of the world.
Yet it can come as lenitive and calm
As comfort from the mother of us all
Sighing you into sleep
Where peace prevails and only soft rains fall.

Song : *Fiona McCleod (William Sharp)*

I have seen all things pass and all things go
Under the shadow of the drifting leaf:
    Green leaf, red leaf, brown leaf,
    Grey leaf blown to and fro,
      Blown to and fro.

I have seen happy dreams rise up and pass
Silent and swift as shadows on the grass;
    Grey shadows of old dreams,
    Grey beauty of old dreams:
      Grey shadows on the grass.

In the Fields : *Charlotte Mew*

Lord, when I look at lovely things which pass,
    Under old trees the shadows of young leaves
Dancing to please the wind along the grass,
    Or the gold stillness of the August sun on the August sheaves;
Can I believe there is a heavenlier world than this?
    And if there is
Will the strange heart of any everlasting thing
    Bring me these dreams that take my breath away?
They come at evening with the home-flying rooks and the scent of
                      hay,
    Over the fields. They come in Spring.

Since I left : *P'ing Li Yü*

      Since I left spring's half gone by.
      All I look at feeds my misery.
Down garden steps plum blossom petals fall, in snow-drifts lie;
    You brush them off and still its snow you're covered by.

The wild geese have flown in yet there's no trace of news.
    The journey is too long even in dreams to dare.
    The bitter grief of leaving is like the spring grass;
        However far you go you find it growing there.

(Translated by Duncan Mackintosh and Alan Ayling)

Song : *Rosa Mulholland*

The silent bird is hid in the boughs,
    The scythe is hid in the corn,
The lazy oxen wink and drowse,
    The grateful sheep are shorn;
Redder and redder burns the rose,
    The lily was ne'er so pale,
Stiller and stiller the river flows
    Along the path to the vale.

A little door is hid in the boughs,
    A face is hiding within;
When birds are silent and oxen drowse
    Why should a maiden spin?
Slower and slower turns the wheel,
    The face turns red and pale,
Brighter and brighter the looks that steal
    Along the path to the vale.

Cossante : *Pero Meogo*

Tell me, daughter, my pretty daughter,
Why you waited by the cold water.
    — It was love, alas!

Tell me, daughter, my lovely daughter,
Why you waited by the cold water.
    — It was love, alas!

I waited, mother, by the cold fountain
While the deer came down the mountain.
    — It was love, alas!

I waited by the cold river mother,
To see the deer, and not for any other.
    — It was love, alas!

You lie, daughter, you lie for your lover,
I never saw deer come down from cover.
    — It was love, alas!

You lie, daughter, for your lover by the fountain,
I never saw deer going up to the mountain.
    — It was love, alas!

(Translated by Yvor Winters)

The Door : *Robert Graves*

When she came suddenly in
It seemed the door could never close again,
Nor even did she close it—she, she—
The room lay open to a visiting sea
Which no door could restrain.

Yet when at last she smiled, tilting her head
To take her leave of me,
Where she had smiled, instead
There was a dark door closing endlessly,
The waves receded.

Carry her over the water : *W. H. Auden*

Carry her over the water,
    And set her down under the tree,
Where the culvers white all day and all night,
    And the winds from every quarter,
Sing agreeably, agreeably, agreeably of love.

Put a gold ring on her finger,
    And press her close to your heart,
While the fish in the lake their snapshots take,
    And the frog, that sanguine singer,
Sings agreeably, agreeably, agreeably of love.

The streets shall all flock to your marriage,
    The houses turn round to look,
The tables and chairs say suitable prayers,
    And the horses drawing your carriage
Sing agreeably, agreeably, agreeably of love.

O my Luve's like a Red, Red Rose :
Robert Burns

O my Luve's like a red, red rose
    That's newly sprung in June:
O my Luve's like the melodie
    That's sweetly played in tune!

As fair art thou, my bonnie lass,
    So deep in luve am I:
And I will luve thee still, my dear,
    Till a' the seas gang dry:

Till a' the seas gang dry, my dear,
    And the rocks melt wi' the sun;
I will luve thee still, my dear,
    While the sands o' life shall run.

And fare thee weel, my only Luve,
    And fare thee weel a while!
And I will come again, my Luve,
    Tho' it were ten thousand mile.

To the Virgins, to Make Much of Time :
Robert Herrick

Gather ye rosebuds while ye may,
    Old Time is still a-flying:
And this same flower that smiles today
    To-morrow will be dying.

The glorious lamp of heaven, the sun,
    The higher he's a-getting,
The sooner will his race be run,
    And nearer he's to setting.

That age is best which is the first,
    When youth and blood are warmer;
But being spent, the worse, and worst
    Times still succeed the former.

Then be not coy, but use your time,
    And while ye may, go marry:
For having lost but once your prime,
    You may for ever tarry.

Down by the Salley Gardens : *W. B. Yeats*

Down by the salley gardens my love and I did meet;
She passed the salley gardens with little snow-white feet.
She bid me take love easy, as the leaves grow on the tree;
But I, being young and foolish, with her would not agree.

In a field by the river my love and I did stand,
And on my leaning shoulder she laid her snow-white hand.
She bid me take life easy, as the grass grows on the weirs;
But I was young and foolish, and now am full of tears.

When I was One-and-Twenty : *A. E. Housman*

When I was one-and-twenty
    I heard a wise man say,
"Give crowns and pounds and guineas
    But not your heart away;
Give pearls away and rubies
    But keep your fancy free."
But I was one-and-twenty,
    No use to talk to me.

When I was one-and-twenty
    I heard him say again,
"The heart out of the bosom
    Was never given in vain;
'Tis paid with sighs a plenty
    And sold for endless rue."
And I am two-and-twenty,
    And oh, 'tis true, 'tis true.

What Thing is Love : *George Peele*

What thing is love, I pray thee tell?
    It is a prickle, it is a sting,
    It is a pretty, pretty thing,
    It is a fire, it is a coal
    Whose flame creeps in at every hole;
    And as my wits can best devise,
    Love's darling lies in ladies' eyes.

Love is a Secret Feeding Fire :
Francis Pilkington

Love is a secret feeding fire that gives all creatures being,
Life to the dead, speech to the dumb, and to the blind man seeing.
And yet in me he contradicts all these his sacred graces,
Seals up my lips, my eyes, my life, and from me ever flying,
Leads me in paths untracked, ungone, and many uncouth places,
Where in despair I beauty curse, curse love and all fair faces.

Starters

Lachrimae : *John Dowland*

Flow, my tears, fall from your springs!
Exiled for ever let me mourn;
Where night's black bird her sad infamy sings,
There let me live forlorn.

Down, vain lights, shine you no more!
No nights are dark enough for those
That in despair their lost fortunes deplore.
Light doth but shame disclose.

Never may my woes be relieved,
Since pity is fled;
And tears and sighs and groans my weary days
Of all joys have deprived.

From the highest spire of contentment
My fortune is thrown:
And fear and grief and pain for my deserts
Are my hopes, since hope is gone.

Hark! you shadows that in darkness dwell,
Learn to contemn light.
Happy, happy they that in hell
Feel not the world's despite.

Ditty : *Edward Herbert*

Tears, flow no more; or if you needs must flow,
Fall yet more slow,
Do not the world invade;
From smaller springs than yours rivers have grown,
And they again a sea have made.
Brackish like you, and which like you hath flown.

Ebb to my heart, and on the burning fires
Of my desires
O let your torrents fall;
From smaller heat than theirs such sparks arise
As into flame converting all,
This world might be but my love's sacrifice.

Yet if the tempests of my sighs so blow,
    You both must flow
  And my desires still burn;
Since that in vain all help my love requires,
    Why may not yet their rages turn
To dry those tears, and to blow out those fires.

"Ah! Sun-flower!" : *William Blake*

Ah! Sun-flower, weary of time,
Who countest the steps of the sun;
Seeking after that sweet golden clime,
Where the traveller's journey is done;

Where the Youth pined away with desire,
And the pale Virgin shrouded in snow,
Arise from their graves, and aspire
Where my Sun-flower wishes to go.

Leaf by Leaf : *Liu K'O Chuang*

Leaf by leaf as light as a butterfly's wing,
    Speck by speck of scarlet in dots so small;
Some people say that God lacks concern for leaf or flower.
    The myriad-formed! The skill that fashioned them all!

See the tree-tops laden with leaf at morning,
    See the branches stripped by the end of day.
Some people say that God undoubtedly cares for leaf and flower.
    The rain has swept them, the wind has blown them away!

(Translated by Duncan Mackintosh and Alan Ayling)

Sonnet : *William Wordsworth*

It is a beauteous evening, calm and free,
The holy time is quiet as a Nun
Breathless with adoration; the broad sun
Is sinking down in its tranquillity;
The gentleness of heaven broods o'er the Sea:
Listen! the mighty Being is awake,
And doth with his eternal motion make
A sound like thunder—everlastingly.

Dear Child! dear Girl! that walkest with me here,
If thou appear untouched by solemn thought,
Thy nature is not therefore less divine:
Thou liest in Abraham's bosom all the year;
And worshipp'st at the Temple's inner shrine,
God being with thee when we know it not.

The Habit of Perfection :
Gerard Manley Hopkins

Elected Silence, sing to me
And beat upon my whorlèd ear,
Pipe me to pastures still and be
The music that I care to hear.

Shape nothing, lips; be lovely-dumb:
It is the shut, the curfew sent
From there where all surrenders come
Which only makes you eloquent.

Be shellèd, eyes, with double dark
And find the uncreated light:
This ruck and reel which you remark
Coils, keeps, and teases simple sight.

Palate, the hutch of tasty lust,
Desire not to be rinsed with wine:
The can must be so sweet, the crust
So fresh that come in fasts divine!

Nostrils, your careless breath that spend
Upon the stir and keep of pride,
What relish shall the censers send
Along the sanctuary side!

O feel-of-primrose hands, O feet
That want the yield of plushy sward,
But you shall walk the golden street
And you unhouse and house the Lord.

And, Poverty, be thou the bride
And now the marriage feast begun,
And lily-coloured clothes provide
Your spouse not laboured-at nor spun.

Song : *Robert Greene*

Sweet are the thoughts that savour of content;
    The quiet mind is richer than a crown;
Sweet are the nights in careless slumber spent;
    The poor estate scorns fortune's angry frown:
Such sweet content, such minds, such sleep, such bliss,
    Beggars enjoy, when princes oft do miss.

The homely house that harbours quiet rest;
    The cottage that affords no pride nor care;
The mean that 'grees with country music best;
    The sweet consort of mirth and music's fare;
Obscuréd life sets down a type of bliss:
A mind content both crown and kingdom is.

Song : *Thomas Deloney*

The primrose in the green forest,
    The violets, they be gay;
The double daisies, and the rest
    That trimly decks the way,
Doth move the spirits with brave delights,
    Who Beauty's darlings be:
With hey tricksy, trim-go-tricksy,
    Under the greenwood tree.

Pastures : *Herbert Read*

We scurry over the pastures
    chasing the windstrewn oak-leaves.

We kiss
the fresh petals of cowslips and primroses.

We discover frog-spawn in the wet ditch.

Starters

The Rainbow : *Walter de la Mare*

I saw the lovely arch
Of rainbow span the sky,
The gold sun burning
As the rain swept by.

In bright ringed solitude
The showery foliage shone
One lovely moment,
And the Bow was gone.

Sudden Shadow :
Samuel Menashe

Crow I scorn you
Caw everywhere
You'll not subdue
This blue air

Maximus : *D. H. Lawrence*

God is older than the sun and the moon
and the eye cannot behold him
nor voice describe him.

But a naked man, a stranger, leaned on the gate
with his cloak over his arm, waiting to be asked in.
So I called him: Come in, if you will!
He came in slowly, and sat down by the hearth.
I said to him: And what is your name?
He looked at me without answer, but such a loveliness
entered me, I smiled to myself, saying: He is God!
So he said: *Hermes!*

God is older than the sun and moon
and the eye cannot behold him
nor the voice describe him:
and still, this is the God Hermes, sitting by my hearth.

Stars : *Peter Levi*

Out of shaking
air and time we came,
at a touching taking
godlike flame,
or like that bird which owns no mate or pair
but hangs forever in the astounded air.

The Starlight Night : *Gerard Manley Hopkins*

Look at the stars! look, look up at the skies!
    O look at all the fire-folk sitting in the air!
    The bright boroughs, the circle-citadels there!
Down in dim woods the diamónd delves! the elves'-eyes!

The grey lawns cold where gold, where quickgold lies!
    Wind-beat whitebeam! airy abeles set on a flare!
    Flake-doves sent floating forth at a farmyard scare!—
Ah well! it is all a purchase, all is a prize.

Buy then! bid then!—What?—Prayer, patience, alms, vows.
Look, look: a May-mess, like on orchard boughs!
    Look! March-bloom, like on mealed-with-yellow sallows!
These are indeed the barn; withindoors house
The shocks. This piece-bright paling shuts the spouse
    Christ home, Christ and his mother and all his hallows.

The Trumpet : *Edward Thomas*

Rise up, rise up,
And, as the trumpet blowing
Chases the dreams of men,
As the dawn glowing
The stars that left unlit
The land and water,
Rise up and scatter
The dew that covers
The print of last night's lovers—
Scatter it, scatter it!
While you are listening
To the clear horn,
Forget, men, everything
On this earth newborn,

17

Starters

Except that it is lovelier
Than any mysteries.
Open your eyes to the air
That has washed the eyes of the stars
Through all the dewy night:
Up with the light,
To the old wars;
Arise, arise!

The Stirring : *John Smith*

I am stirring. I have slept.
God! How long I have slept.
Can you hear me stirring,
Like wings in a chrysalis?

I am stirring. My eyes are opening,
Opening as they opened first upon the world.
I am become Quick. I am shedding the death
That has been swaddling me. Soft, maggot-death!

Now I hear sounds that have been shut from me.
Can you hear them? I must make you hear them,
The sounds, the words. For the stone of dumbness
Has rolled from my cave mouth.

I am stirring. Look at me! Look!
At my green shining as I seethe and rise,
As I uncurl and stretch up till my gaze
Whips the white air to a cobalt firmament.

Now you will see me as I march about;
I will festoon the world with pennants and banners,
Running before you with visions and sweet music,
Racing before you with laughters in my mouth.

I have slept, but now, at last I am stirring,
Like a windmill, like the glittering wind itself.
Oh all you sleepers and dreamers, come with me. Wake.
Wake with me. Stir with me. Now.

Conversation
between Courses

Please : *Michael Burn*

O God, do something worldly for us!
O, load us with a very large sum of money
Now,
And in any reliable currency
Allow
Us to be surprised. Fill up our dustbin
With packages of undevalued
Yen,
Reichsmark, or the more humbly pursued
Pound.
Begin
Each day with the
Sound
Of a not small cheque.
Let
Paul Get-
-ty and Barbara Hutton take a fancy to either or both of us.
Thrus-
-t several remunerative and gay
Temptat-
-ions in our way.
Such as a
Venice palazzo with a whale-
-scale swimpool, and a
Merc,
Or two Mercs. Arrange for my
Work
To be high-
-ly app-
-lauded everywhere, and re-
-warded beyond its merits. Snap
Thy magnificent fingers, be
Not skimping with largesse,
Tax-free;
For example gold
Francs
And from untold
Swiss rolls and credits in countless
Banks,
O God, withhold
Not
O not withhold Thy hand.
But

21

Conversation between Courses

With such mundane meaningless things, Almighty, cover us thick
Ageing babes-in-the-wood, and
Cover us quick!

Scratch : *Jonathan Graham Burton*

He sat scratching,
    he was good at scratching,
he did a lot of scratching.
    He itched as well.
He sat itching,
    He was even better at itching,
He did even more itching than scratching.
    He sat itching and scratching,
he sat scratching and itching.
    He hated people who didn't scratch.
He sat watching people to see if they
    scratched or not, like he did.
He never washed in case it stopped him
    itching and scratching.
People told him he was smelly,
    he wasn't smelly,
he was itchy and scratchy.
    He praised the flea,
the symbol of itching and scratching.
    He wondered why fleas didn't itch or scratch.
Or maybe they did.
    His mother said he would die of
itching and scratching or chewing string.
    He liked chewing string.
He sat chewing string.
    He was good at chewing string.
He chewed a lot of string.
    He sat scratching, itching and chewing string.
        It was good to be normal.

Waking : *Michi-nobu*

Although I know the gentle night
    Will surely follow morn,
Yet, when I'm wakened by the sun,
    Turn over, stretch and yawn —
    How I detest the dawn!

(Translated by William N. Porter)

A Baby's Epitaph : *Anon*

A muvver was barfin' 'er biby one night,
The youngest of ten and a tiny young mite,
The muvver was poor and the biby was thin,
Only a skelington covered in skin;
The muvver turned rahnd for the soap orf the rack,
She was but a moment, but when she turned back,
The biby was gorn; and in anguish she cried,
"Oh, where is my biby?" — The angels replied:

"Your biby 'as fell dahn the plug-'ole,
Your biby 'as gorn dahn the plug;
The poor little thing was so skinny and thin
'E oughter been barfed in a jug;
Your biby is perfeckly 'appy,
'E won't need a barf any more,
Your biby 'as fell dahn the plug-'ole,
Not lorst, but gorn before."

Miss Twye : *Gavin Ewart*

Miss Twye was soaping her breasts in her bath
When she heard behind her a meaning laugh
And to her amazement she discovered
A wicked man in the bathroom cupboard.

The Lesser Lynx : *E. V. Rieu*

The laughter of the Lesser Lynx
    Is often insincere:
It pays to be polite, he thinks,
    If Royalty is near.

Conversation between Courses

So when the Lion steals his food
    Or kicks him from behind,
He smiles, of course—but oh, the rude
    Remarks that cross his mind.

Jumbo : *Stevie Smith*

Jumbo, Jumbo, Jumbo, darling, Jumbo come to Mother.
But Jumbo wouldn't, he was a dog who simply wouldn't bother
An ugly beast he was with drooping guts and filthy skin,
It was quite wonderful how "mother" loved the ugly thing.

Birds of a Feather : *Nursery Rhyme*

Birds of a feather flock together
And so will pigs and swine;
Rats and mice shall have their choice,
And so shall I have mine.

The English are so Nice! : *D. H. Lawrence*

The English are so nice
so awfully nice
they are the nicest people in the world.
And what's more, they're very nice about being nice
about your being nice as well!
if you're not nice they soon make you feel it.

Americans and French and Germans and so on
they're all very well
but they're not *really* nice, you know.
They're not nice in *our* sense of the word, are they now?

That's why one doesn't have to take them seriously.
We must be nice to them, of course,
of course, naturally—
But it doesn't really matter what you say to them,
they don't really understand
you can just say anything to them:
be nice, you know, just nice
but you must never take them seriously, they wouldn't understand,
just be nice, you know! oh, fairly nice,
not too nice of course, they take advantage
but nice enough, just nice enough
to let them feel they're not quite as nice as they might be.

Cousin Nancy : *T. S. Eliot*

Miss Nancy Ellicott
Strode across the hills and broke them,
Rode across the hills and broke them—
The barren New England Hills—
Riding to hounds
Over the cow-pasture.

Miss Nancy Ellicott smoked
And danced all the modern dances;
And her aunts were not sure how they felt about it,
But they knew that it was modern.

Upon the glazen shelves kept watch
Matthew and Waldo, guardians of the faith,
The army of unalterable law.

Agricultural Caress : *John Betjeman*

Keep me from Thelma's sister Pearl!
She puts my senses in a whirl,
Weakens my knees and keeps me waiting
Until my heart stops palpitating.

The debs may turn disdainful backs
On Pearl's uncouth mechanic slacks,
And outraged see the fire that lies
And smoulders in her long-lashed eyes.

Conversation between Courses

Have they such weather-freckled features,
The smooth sophisticated creatures?
Ah, not to them such limbs belong,
Such animal movements sure and strong,

Such arms to take a man and press
In agricultural caress
His head to hers, and hold him there
Deep buried in her chestnut hair.

God shrive me from this morning lust
For supple farm girls: if you must,
Send the cold daughter of an earl—
But spare me Thelma's sister Pearl!

Jeanie with the Light-Brown Hair :
Stephen C. Foster

I dream of Jeanie with the light-brown hair
    Borne like a vapour on the summer air;
I see her tripping where the bright streams play,
    Happy as the daisies that dance on her way;
Many were the wild notes her merry voice would pour
    Many were the blithe birds that warbled them o'er.

I long for Jeanie with the day-dawn smile,
    Radiant in gladness, warm with winning guile;
I hear her melodies, like joys gone by,
    Sighing round my heart o'er the fond hopes that die—
Sighing like the night wind, and sobbing like the rain,
    Wailing for the lost one that comes not again.

I sigh for Jeanie, but her light form stray'd
    Far from the fond hearts around her native glade,
Her smiles have vanish'd, and her sweet songs flown,
    Flitting like the dreams that have cheered us and gone.
Now nodding wild-flow'rs may wither on the shore,
    But her gentle fingers will cull them no more.

Upon Julia's Clothes : *Robert Herrick*

Whenas in silks my Julia goes,
Then, then, methinks, how sweetly flows
The liquefaction of her clothes!

Next, when I cast mine eyes and see
That brave vibration each way free,
—O how that glittering taketh me!

To a Lady, asking him how long he would love her : *George Etherege*

It is not, Celia, in our power
To say how long our love will last;
It may be we within this hour
May lose those joys we now do taste;
The blessed, that immortal be,
From change in love are only free.

Then, since we mortal lovers are,
Ask not how long our love will last;
But while it does, let us take care
Each minute be with pleasure passed:
Were it not madness to deny
To live because we're sure to die?

The Sea said "Come" : *Emily Dickinson*

The Sea said "Come" to the Brook,
The Brook said "Let me grow!"
The Sea said "Then you will be a sea—
I want a brook, Come now!"

Suzanne : *William Carlos Williams*

Brother Paul! look!
—but he rushes to a different
window.
The moon!

I heard shrieks and thought:
What's that?

Conversation between Courses

That's just Suzanne
talking to the moon!
Pounding on the window
with both fists:

    Paul!   Paul!

—and talking to the moon.
Shrieking
and pounding on the glass
with both fists!

Brother Paul! the moon!

Yet Gentle will the Griffin Be : *Vachel Lindsay*

(What Grandpa told the Children)

The moon? It is a griffin's egg
Hatching tomorrow night.
And how the little boys will watch
With shouting and delight
To see him break the shell and stretch
And creep across the sky.
The boys will laugh. The little girls,
I fear, may hide and cry.
Yet gentle will the griffin be,
Most decorous and fat,
And walk up to the milky way
And lap it like a cat.

Pets : *Daniel Pettiward*

Once we had a little retriever
But it bit our beaver
Which had already bitten
Our Siamese kitten
Which had not been pleasant
To our golden pheasant.
The pheasant took a dislike to Laura,
Our Angora,
Who left her hairs
On the Louis Quinze chairs

And her paws
On one of our jackdaws
Who were not at all nice
To our white mice
Who were openly rude
To our bantam brood
Whose beaks were too sharp
For our golden carp
Who were on rotten terms
With our silk-worms
Who were swallowed up
By our retriever pup
Who consequently died
With all that silk inside.
Then we knew we'd have to buy
Something so high
And stout and strong it
Would let nobody wrong it;
So we purchased a hyena
Which, though it ate my sister Lena
And some embroidery off the shelf,
Remained intact itself
And has not yet died
So that our choice was justified.

Conversation between Courses

Nobody loses all the time : *e.e.cummings*

nobody loses all the time

i had an uncle named
Sol who was a born failure and
nearly everybody said he should have gone
into vaudeville perhaps my Uncle Sol could
sing McCann He Was A Diver on Xmas Eve like Hell Itself which
may or may not account for the fact that my Uncle

Sol indulged in that possibly most inexcusable
of all to use a highfalootin phrase
luxuries that is or to
wit farming and be
it needlessly
added

my Uncle Sol's farm
failed because the chickens
ate the vegetables so
my Uncle Sol had a
chicken farm till the
skunks ate the chickens when

my Uncle Sol
had a skunk farm but
the skunks caught cold and
died and so
my Uncle Sol imitated the
skunks in a subtle manner

or by drowning himself in the watertank
but somebody who'd given my Uncle Sol a Victor
Victrola and records while he lived presented to
him upon the auspicious occasion of his decease a
scrumptious not to mention splendiferous funeral with
tall boys in black gloves and flowers and everything and

i remember we all cried like the Missouri
when my Uncle Sol's coffin lurched because
somebody pressed a button
(and down went
my Uncle
Sol

and started a worm farm)

As I was going to Derby : *Nursery Rhyme*

As I was going to Derby,
    Upon a market day,
I met the finest ram, sir,
    That ever was fed on hay.

This ram was fat behind, sir,
    This ram was fat before,
This ram was ten yards high, sir,
    Indeed he was no more.

The wool upon his back, sir,
    Reached up into the sky,
The eagles built their nests there,
    For I heard the young ones cry.

The space between the horns, sir,
    Was as far as man could reach,
And there they built a pulpit,
    But no one in it preached.

This ram had four legs to walk upon,
    This ram had four legs to stand,
And every leg he had, sir,
    Stood on an acre of land.

Now the man that fed the ram, sir,
    He fed him twice a day,
And each time that he fed him, sir,
    He ate a rick of hay.

The man that killed this ram, sir,
    Was up to his knees in blood,
And the boy that held the pail, sir,
    Was carried away in the flood.

Conversation between Courses

Indeed sir, it's the truth, sir,
  For I never was taught to lie,
And if you go to Derby, sir,
  You may eat a bit of the pie.

I'm a Shrimp! I'm a Shrimp! : *Robert Brough*

I'm a shrimp! I'm a shrimp! Of diminutive size.
Inspect my antennae, and look at my eyes;
I'm a natural syphon, when dipped in a cup,
For I drain the contents to the latest drop up.
I care not for craw-fish, I heed not the prawn,
From a flavour especial my fame has been drawn;
Nor e'en to the crab or the lobster do yield,
When I'm properly cook'd and efficiently peeled.
Quick! Quick! pile the coals—let your saucepan be deep,
For the weather is warm, and I'm sure not to keep;
Off, off with my head—split my shell into three—
I'm a shrimp! I'm a shrimp—to be eaten with tea.

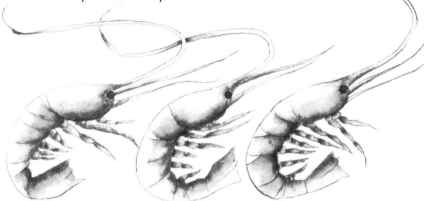

A Pot poured out : *Samuel Menashe*

A pot poured out
Fulfils its spout

Jog On, Jog On : *William Shakespeare*

Jog on, jog on, the foot-path way,
  And merrily hent the stile-a:
A merry heart goes all the day,
  Your sad tires in a mile-a.

The Main Course

Wonder : *Thomas Traherne*

How like an Angel came I down!
    How bright are all things here!
When first among His works I did appear
    O how their Glory me did crown!
The world resembled his *Eternity*,
    In which my soul did walk;
And every thing that I did see
    Did with me talk.

The skies in their magnificence,
    The lively, lovely air,
Oh how divine, how soft, how sweet, how fair!
    The stars did entertain my sense,
And all the works of God, so bright and pure,
    So rich and great did seem,
As if they ever must endure
    In my esteem.

A native health and innocence
    Within my bones did grow,
And while my God did all his Glories show,
    I felt a vigour in my sense
That was all Spirit. I within did flow
    With seas of life, like wine;
I nothing in the world did know
    But 'twas divine.

Harsh ragged objects were concealed,
    Oppressions, tears and cries,
Sins, griefs, complaints, dissensions, weeping eyes
    Were hid, and only things revealed
Which heavenly Spirits and the Angels prize.
    The state of Innocence
And bliss, not trades and poverties,
    Did fill my sense.

The streets were paved with golden stones,
    The boys and girls were mine,
Oh how did all their lovely faces shine!
    The sons of men were holy ones,
In joy and beauty they appeared to me,
    And every thing which here I found,
While like an angel I did see,
    Adorned the ground.

The Main Course

Rich diamond and pearl and gold
    In every place was seen;
Rare splendours, yellow, blue, red, white and green,
    Mine eyes did everywhere behold.
Great Wonders clothed with glory did appear,
    Amazement was my bliss,
That and my wealth was everywhere;
    No joy to this!

Cursed and devised proprieties,
    With envy, avarice
And fraud, those friends that spoil even paradise,
    Flew from the splendour of mine eyes.
And so did hedges, ditches, limits, bounds,
    I dreamed not aught of those,
But wandered over all men's grounds,
    And found repose.

Proprieties themselves were mine,
    And hedges ornaments;
Walls, boxes, coffers, and their rich contents
    Did not divide my joys, but all combine.
Clothes, ribbons, jewels, laces, I esteemed
    My joys by others worn:
For me they all to wear them seemed
    When I was born.

God's Grandeur : *Gerard Manley Hopkins*

The world is charged with the grandeur of God.
    It will flame out, like shining from shook foil;
    It gathers to a greatness, like the ooze of oil
Crushed. Why do men then now not reck his rod?
Generations have trod, have trod, have trod;
    And all is seared with trade; bleared, smeared with toil;
    And wears man's smudge and shares man's smell: the soil
Is bare now, nor can foot feel, being shod.

And for all this, nature is never spent;
    There lives the dearest freshness deep down things;
And though the last lights off the black West went
    Oh, morning, at the brown brink eastward springs—
Because the Holy Ghost over the bent
    World broods with warm breast and with ah! bright wings.

Day of these Days : *Laurie Lee*

Such a morning it is when love
leans through geranium windows
and calls with a cockerel's tongue.

When red-haired girls scamper like roses
over the rain-green grass,
and the sun drips honey.

When hedgerows grow venerable,
berries dry black as blood,
and holes suck in their bees.

Such a morning it is when mice
run whispering from the church,
dragging dropped ears of harvest.

When the partridge draws back his spring
and shoots like a buzzing arrow
over grained and mahogany fields.

When no table is bare,
and no breast dry,
and the tramp feeds off ribs of rabbit.

Such a day it is when time
piles up the hills like pumpkins,
and the streams run golden.

When all men smell good,
and the cheeks of girls
are as baked bread to the mouth.

As bread and beanflowers
the touch of their lips,
and their white teeth sweeter than cucumbers.

The Main Course

The Window : *Peter Yates*

A door bangs faintly in the house;
The curtains stir like falling leaves;
A tilted glass unfolds the sky.
The grief that seemed your only dress
Slips off as softly as a sigh.

The early rose is born to bleed,
And reach through pain its secret joy:
Such things true lovers understand;
And like a little pulsing bird
Your risen breast comes to my hand.

Blown on a breath of Summer air
The scented garden creeps inside;
And fitful as a butterfly
The sunlight with its golden tongue
Touches us briefly where we lie.

Welcome, My Woman! : *Nazim Hikmet*

Welcome, my dear wife, welcome!
You must be tired:
how can I wash your little feet?
I have neither a silver basin nor rose water.
You must be thirsty:
I have no iced sherbert to offer you.
You must be hungry:
I cannot give you a banquet
  laid on a white embroidered cloth—
  my room is as poor as my country.

Welcome, my dear woman, welcome!
Soon as you stepped into my room,
  the forty-year-old concrete became grass;
when you smiled
  the iron bars of the window blossomed with roses,
when you wept
  my hands were filled with pearls.
My cell has become as rich as my heart
  as bright as liberty.

Welcome, my own, welcome, welcome!

(Translated by Taner Baybars)

38

This Small Hostility : *Philip Hobsbaum*

Well, we were nicely settled in our flat,
Light bulbs inserted, kitchen cabinets fixed,
Carpets down, one or two pictures up
Much as we wanted in the place we'd wanted.
Yet on our wedding night she went out, found
Black on the floor a beetle lying flat,
Its legs waving feebly in the air.
Still beetles don't mean much. We weren't defeated.

The garden glittered in the August sun
Pleasant to look at when, half under ground,
Flit pump in hand I sprayed the tentative beetles,
Leaving small wet collapses down the hall.
The beetles died, but in her bath one day,
Swimming with all eight legs, she found a spider.

I'd chase the flying spiders up the wall,
Over the ceiling. They dropped without a trace.
They had no right, I felt, where we were living.
When we had killed the spiders came the flies,
Buzzing into our hair, tangling with food.
I'd read in bed and flit them as they were flying.

And then the mice. A nice young poet once
Came down to see us. While we ate they rattled
Along the skirting-board, clumped in the hall.
Finally one rushed out and over his shoe.
What's that? A mouse? he said. Next night
I trod on one lying dead, or perhaps I'd killed it.

I hate killing, even insects. So they won,
Not gradually but all at once. Late
She made some tea, saw rice grains on the floor,
Stooped to examine when they glinted whitely,
Found small white worms. I came at length to look,
But what I saw were a dozen, twenty maggots.

Swept them into a pan, opened the back door
Torch in hand to see by. What I saw—
The steps were white with maggots, soft and writhing,
Seeming to hump in the shaking beam of my torch.
They poured like liquid down. I slammed the door.
They crept under the door into the kitchen.

The Main Course

I sat on the sink. I had to work this out.
They knew just where to go and how to get there.
I'd rather have had a tiger in the kitchen.
Unclean, unclean. She said put pails to boil,
Pour boiling water on them. And they sizzled
Under the gallons of water crashing down
Over the floor cascading them into the drains.
We poured and swept and mopped up until morning.

And so we left. The creatures have it now,
The flat we meant to stay in. Beetles can eat
Whatever crumbs the mice leave, let the spiders
Trap what torpid flies hatched out. Leave all
To rot as food for maggots and for mildew.
There were some cupboards that I did not open.
We left the flat to insects and to fever.

The New House : *Edward Thomas*

Now first, as I shut the door,
I was alone
In the new house; and the wind
Began to moan.

Old at once was the house,
And I was old;
My ears were teased with the dread
Of what was foretold,

Nights of storm, days of mist, without end;
Sad days when the sun
Shone in vain: old griefs, and griefs
Not yet begun.

All was foretold me; naught
Could I foresee;
But I learnt how the wind would sound
After these things should be.

Disillusion at Ten o'Clock : *Wallace Stevens*

The houses are haunted
By white night-gowns.
None are green,
Or purple with green rings,
Or green with yellow rings,
Or yellow with blue rings.
None of them are strange,
With socks of lace
And beaded ceintures.
People are not going
To dream of baboons and periwinkles.
Only, here and there, an old sailor,
Drunk and asleep in his boots,
Catches tigers
In red weather.

Day : *John Smith*

Assembles day. Watch now
Who have not watched, how
It goes. Not as you thought,
Not at all. First, caught,
As a child birthed in a caul,
Witness a dazed, struggling ball,
The sun. It has to fight
Up out of the ground, light
Diffused, not brilliant, grey.
Nevertheless it assembles day.

Now it puts it together bit by bit
Like a complex sentence, knit
By extravagant syntax. A tree
Untangles itself, breaks free
Of the dark, discovers green.
Nearby a pond has the sheen
Of an opal; its eye
Stares up at a reflected pond, the sky.
Olive grey at the edge, rushes
Stain the mauve blur of elder bushes.

The Main Course

Some of the dark does not rise;
Clouds go but the hill lies
Humped still. Now, sound
Falls in little spurts onto the ground
Out of the space above it, out of air;
Wings are not visible but birds are there.
With relentless beaks they peck the shawl
Of night to pieces. They let fall
Skein after skein; the rags
Drift in tatters where shadow lags.

You have been watching, but
You have not seen. Now shut
Your eyes again; night is back.
And how does day assemble from that black?
First, caught as a child...
Already the conceit has you beguiled.
Very well, look! Take your hand
Away from your face. The land
Lies like a finished jigsaw. As an eyelash trembles,
As fast, as slow, day assembles.

A Carol for Christmas Day : *William Byrd*

An earthly tree a heavenly fruit it bare;
 A case of clay contained a crown immortal,
A crown of crowns, a King, whose cost and care
 Redeemed poor man, whose race before was thrall
To death, to doom, to pains of everlasting,
By his sweet death, scorns, stripes, and often fasting.
  Cast off all doubtful care,
   Exile and banish tears,
  To joyful news divine
   Lend us your listening ears.

A Star above the stars, a Sun of light,
 Whose blessed beams this wretched earth bespread
With hope of heaven and of God's Son the sight,
 Which in our flesh and sinful soul lay dead.
O faith, O hope, O joys renowned for ever,
O lively life, that deathless shall persever.
  Cast off all doubtful care,
   Exile and banish tears,
  To joyful news divine
   Lend us your listening ears.

Then let us sing the lullabies of sleep
    To this sweet Babe, born to awake us all
From drowsy sin, that made old Adam weep,
    And by his fault gave to mankind the fall.
For lo, this day, the birth day, day of days,
Summons our songs to give him laud and praise.
        Cast off all doubtful care,
          Exile and banish tears,
        To joyful news divine
          Lend us your listening ears.

Joseph was an Old Man : *Anon*

Joseph was an old man,
    And an old man was he,
When he wedded Mary
    In the land of Galilee.

Joseph and Mary walked
    Through an orchard good,
Where was cherries and berries
    So red as any blood.

Joseph and Mary walked
    Through an orchard green,
Where was berries and cherries
    As thick as might be seen.

O then bespoke Mary
    So meek and so mild,
"Pluck me one cherry, Joseph,
    For I am with child."

O then bespoke Joseph
    With words so unkind,
"Let him pluck thee a cherry
    That brought thee with child."

O then bespoke the babe
    Within his mother's womb,
"Bow down then the tallest tree
    For my mother to have some."

The Main Course

Then bowed down the highest tree
　　Unto his mother's hand:
Then she cried, "See, Joseph,
　　I have cherries at command!"

O then bespake Joseph—
　　"I have done Mary wrong;
But cheer up, my dearest,
　　And be not cast down.

O eat your cherries, Mary,
　　O eat your cherries now;
O eat your cherries, Mary,
　　That grow upon the bough."

Then Mary plucked a cherry
　　As red as the blood;
Then Mary went home
　　With her heavy load.

Ballad of the Bread Man : *Charles Causley*

Mary stood in the kitchen
Baking a loaf of bread.
An angel flew in through the window.
We've a job for you, he said.

God in his big gold heaven,
Sitting in his big blue chair,
Wanted a mother for his little son.
Suddenly saw you there.

44

Mary shook and trembled,
It isn't true what you say.
Don't say that, said the angel.
The baby's on its way.

Joseph was in the workshop
Planing a piece of wood.
The old man's past it, the neighbours said
That girl's been up to no good.

And who was that elegant feller,
They said, in the shiny gear?
The things they said about Gabriel
Were hardly fit to hear.

Mary never answered,
Mary never replied.
She kept the information,
Like the baby, safe inside.

It was election winter.
They went to vote in town.
When Mary found her time had come
The hotels let her down.

The baby was born in an annexe
Next to the local pub.
At midnight, a delegation
Turned up from the Farmers' Club.

They talked about an explosion
That cracked a hole in the sky,
Said they'd been sent to the Lamb & Flag
To see God come down from on high.

A few days later a bishop
And a five-star general were seen
With the head of an African country
In a bullet-proof limousine.

We've come, they said, with tokens
For the little boy to choose.
Told the tale about war and peace
In the television news.

The Main Course

After them came the soldiers
With rifle and bomb and gun,
Looking for enemies of the state.
The family had packed and gone.

When they got back to the village
The neighbours said, to a man,
That boy will never be one of us,
Though he does what he blessed well can.

He went round to all the people
A paper crown on his head.
Here is some bread from my father.
Take, eat, he said.

Nobody seemed very hungry.
Nobody seemed to care.
Nobody saw the god in himself
Quietly standing there.

He finished up in the papers.
He came to a very bad end.
He was charged with bringing the living to life.
No man was that prisoner's friend.

There's only one kind of punishment
To fit that kind of a crime.
They rigged a trial and shot him dead.
They were only just in time.

They lifted the young man by the leg,
They lifted him by the arm,
They locked him in a cathedral
In case he came to harm.

They stored him safe as water
Under seven rocks.
One Sunday morning he burst out
Like a jack-in-the-box.

Through the town he went walking.
He showed them the holes in his head.
Now do you want any loaves? he cried.
Not today, they said.

46

A New Year Carol : *Anon*

Here we bring new water
    from the well so clear,
For to worship God with,
    this happy New Year.
Sing levy dew, sing levy dew,
    the water and the wine;
The seven bright gold wires
    and the bugles that do shine.

Sing reign of Fair Maid,
    with gold upon her toe, —
Open you the West Door,
    and turn the Old Year go.

Sing reign of Fair Maid
    with gold upon her chin, —
Open you the East Door,
    and let the New Year in.
Sing levy dew, sing levy dew,
    the water and the wine;
The seven bright gold wires
    and the bugles that do shine.

Ozymandias : *Percy Bysshe Shelley*

I met a traveller from an antique land
Who said: Two vast and trunkless legs of stone
Stand in the desert...Near them, on the sand,
Half sunk, a shattered visage lies, whose frown,
And wrinkled lip, and sneer of cold command,
Tell that its sculptor well those passions read
Which yet survive, stamped on these lifeless things,
The hand that mocked them, and the heart that fed:
And on the pedestal these words appear:
"My name is Ozymandias, king of kings:
Look on my works, ye Mighty, and despair!"
Nothing beside remains. Round the decay
Of that colossal wreck, boundless and bare
The lone and level sands stretch far away.

The Main Course

The Second Coming : *W. B. Yeats*

Turning and turning in the widening gyre
The falcon cannot hear the falconer;
Things fall apart; the centre cannot hold;
Mere anarchy is loosed upon the world,
The blood-dimmed tide is loosed, and everywhere
The ceremony of innocence is drowned;
The best lack all conviction, while the worst
Are full of passionate intensity.

Surely some revelation is at hand;
Surely the Second Coming is at hand.
The Second Coming! Hardly are those words out
When a vast image out of *Spiritus Mundi*
Troubles my sight: somewhere in sands of the desert
A shape with lion body and the head of a man,
A gaze blank and pitiless as the sun,
Is moving its slow thighs, while all about it
Reel shadows of the indignant desert birds.
The darkness drops again; but now I know
That twenty centuries of stony sleep
Were vexed to nightmare by a rocking cradle,
And what rough beast, its hour come round at last,
Slouches towards Bethlehem to be born?

The Mockery of Life : *Wilfrid Scawen Blunt*

God! What a mockery is this life of ours!
Cast forth in blood and pain from our mother's womb,
Most like an excrement, and weeping showers
Of senseless tears: unreasoning, naked, dumb,
The symbol of all weakness and the sum:
Our very life a sufferance. — Presently,
Grown sronger, we must fight for standing-room
Upon the earth, and the bare liberty
To breathe and move. We crave the right to toil.

We push, we strive, we jostle with the rest.
We learn new courage, stifle our old fears,
Stand with stiff backs, take part in every broil.
It may be that we love, that we are blest.
It may be, for a little space of years,
We conquer fate and half forget our tears.

And then fate strikes us. First our joys decay.
Youth, with its pleasures, is a tale soon told.
We grow a little poorer day by day.
Old friendships falter. Loves grow strangely cold.
In vain we shift our hearts to a new hold
And barter joy for joy, the less for less.
We doubt our strength, our wisdom, and our gold.
We stand alone, as in a wilderness
Of doubts and terrors. Then, if we be wise,
We make our terms with fate and, while we may,
Sell our life's last sad remnant for a hope.
And it is wisdom thus to close our eyes.
But for the foolish, those who cannot pray,
What else remains of their dark horoscope
But a tall tree and courage and a rope?

And who shall tell what ignominy death
Has yet in store for us; what abject fears
Even for the best of us; what fights for breath;
What sobs, what supplications, what wild tears;
What impotence of soul against despairs
Which blot out reason?—The last trembling thought
Of each poor brain, as dissolution nears,
Is not of fair life lost, of Heaven bought
And glory won. 'Tis not the thought of grief;
Of friends deserted; loving hearts which bleed;
Wives, sisters, children who around us weep.

But only a mad clutching for relief
From physical pain, importunate Nature's need;
The search as for a womb where we may creep
Back from the world, to hide,—perhaps to sleep.

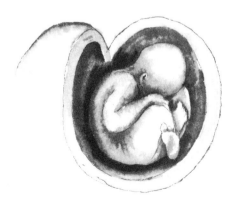

The Main Course

Fragment : *Hartley Coleridge*

What is the life of man? From first to last,
Its only substance, the unbeing past!
The infant smiling in its sleep must dream
Of something past, before the vexing beam
Of daylight smote the unaccustom'd eye,
Ere the faint mother heard its first faint cry;
Lull'd in its rocking nest, it seeks in vain
For what has been, and ne'er can be again.
The child, through every maze of wakening lore,
Hunts the huge shadow of what was before,
Sees his old toys in misty phantoms glide,
'Twixt hope and dim oblivion magnified;
As oft on misty hills huge spectres run,
And stalk gigantic from the setting sun—
Still urging onward to the world unseen,
Yet wishing, hoping nought, but what has been.
But what *has* been? But *how,* and *when,* and *where?*
Was there a time, when, wandering in the air,
The living spark existed, yet unnamed,
Unfixt, unqualitied, unlaw'd, unclaim'd,
A drop of being, in the infinite sea,
Whose only duty, essence, was to be?
Or must we seek it, where all things we find,
In the sole purpose of creative mind?
Or did it serve, in form of stone or plant,
Or weaving worm, or the wise politic ant,
Its weary bondage—ere the moment came,
When the weak spark should mount into a flame?

Ode to a Nightingale : *John Keats*

My heart aches, and a drowsy numbness pains
   My sense, as though of hemlock I had drunk,
Or emptied some dull opiate to the drains
   One minute past, and Lethe-wards had sunk:
'Tis not through envy of thy happy lot,
   But being too happy in thy happiness,—
      That thou, light-wingèd Dryad of the trees,
      In some melodious plot
Of beechen green, and shadows numberless,
   Singest of summer in full-throated ease.

O, for a draught of vintage! that hath been
  Cool'd a long age in the deep-delvèd earth,
Tasting of Flora and the country green,
  Dance, and Provençal song, and sunburnt mirth!
O for a beaker full of the warm South,
  Full of the true, the blushful Hippocrene,
    With beaded bubbles winking at the brim,
      And purple-stainèd mouth;
That I might drink, and leave the world unseen,
  And with thee fade away into the forest dim:

Fade far away, dissolve, and quite forget
  What thou among the leaves hast never known,
The weariness, the fever, and the fret
  Here, where men sit and hear each other groan;
Where palsy shakes a few, sad, last gray hairs,
  Where youth grows pale, and spectre-thin, and dies;
    Where but to think is to be full of sorrow
      And leaden-eyed despairs;
Where Beauty cannot keep her lustrous eyes,
  Or new Love pine at them beyond to-morrow.

Away! away! for I will fly to thee,
  Not charioted by Bacchus and his pards,
But on the viewless wings of Poesy,
  Though the dull brain perplexes and retards:
Already with thee! tender is the night,
  And haply the Queen-Moon is on her throne,
    Cluster'd around by all her starry Fays;
      But here there is no light,
Save what from heaven is with the breezes blown
  Through verdurous glooms and winding mossy ways.

I cannot see what flowers are at my feet,
  Nor what soft incense hangs upon the boughs,
But, in embalmèd darkness, guess each sweet
  Wherewith the seasonable month endows
The grass, the thicket, and the fruit-tree wild;
  White hawthorn, and the pastoral eglantine;
    Fast fading violets cover'd up in leaves;
      And mid-May's eldest child,
The coming musk-rose, full of dewy wine,
  The murmurous haunt of flies on summer eves.

The Main Course

Darkling I listen; and for many a time
  I have been half in love with easeful Death,
Call'd him soft names in many a musèd rhyme,
  To take into the air my quiet breath;
Now more than ever seems it rich to die,
  To cease upon the midnight with no pain,
    While thou art pouring forth thy soul abroad
     In such an ecstasy!
Still wouldst thou sing, and I have ears in vain—
  To thy high requiem become a sod.

Thou wast not born for death, immortal Bird!
  No hungry generations tread thee down;
The voice I hear this passing night was heard
  In ancient days by emperor and clown:
Perhaps the self-same song that found a path
  Through the sad heart of Ruth, when sick for home,
    She stood in tears amid the alien corn;
     The same that oft-times hath
Charm'd magic casements, opening on the foam
  Of perilous seas, in faery lands forlorn.

Forlorn! the very word is like a bell
  To toll me back from thee to my sole self!
Adieu! the fancy cannot cheat so well
  As she is fam'd to do, deceiving elf.
Adieu! adieu! thy plaintive anthem fades
  Past the near meadows, over the still stream,
    Up the hill-side: and now 'tis buried deep
     In the next valley-glades:
Was it a vision, or a waking dream?
  Fled is that music:—Do I wake or sleep?

The Groundhog : *Richard Eberhart*

In June, amid the golden fields,
I saw a groundhog lying dead.
Dead lay he; my senses shook,
And mind outshot our naked frailty.
There lowly in the vigorous summer
His form began its senseless change,
And made my senses waver dim
Seeing nature ferocious in him.
Inspecting close his maggots' might
And seething cauldron of his being,
Half with loathing, half with a strange love,
I poked him with an angry stick.
The fever arose, became a flame
And Vigour circumscribed the skies,
Immense energy in the sun,
And through my frame a sunless trembling.
My stick had done nor good nor harm.
Then stood I silent in the day
Watching the object, as before;
And kept my reverence for knowledge
Trying for control, to be still,
To quell the passion of the blood;
Until I had bent down on my knees
Praying for joy in the sight of decay.
And so I left; and I returned
In Autumn strict of eye, to see
The sap gone out of the groundhog,
But the bony sodden hulk remained.
But the year had lost its meaning,
And in intellectual chains
I lost both love and loathing,
Mured up in the wall of wisdom.
Another summer took the fields again
Massive and burning, full of life,
But when I chanced upon the spot
There was only a little hair left,
And bones bleaching in the sunlight
Beautiful as architecture;
I watched them like a geometer,
And cut a walking stick from a birch.
It has been three years, now.
There is no sign of the groundhog.
I stood there in the whirling summer,

The Main Course

My hand capped a withered heart,
And thought of China and of Greece,
Of Alexander in his tent;
Of Montaigne in his tower,
Of Saint Theresa in her wild lament.

View of a Pig : *Ted Hughes*

The pig lay on a barrow dead.
It weighed, they said, as much as three men.
Its eyes closed, pink white eyelashes.
Its trotters stuck straight out.

Such weight and thick pink bulk
Set in death seemed not just dead.
It was less than lifeless, further off.
It was like a sack of wheat.

I thumped it without feeling remorse.
One feels guilty insulting the dead,
Walking on graves. But this pig
Did not seem able to accuse.

It was too dead. Just so much
A poundage of lard and pork.
Its last dignity had entirely gone.
It was not a figure of fun.

Too dead now to pity.
To remember its life, din, stronghold
Of earthly pleasure as it had been,
Seemed a false effort, and off the point.

Too deadly factual. Its weight
Oppressed me — how could it be moved?
And the trouble of cutting it up!
The gash in its throat was shocking, but not pathetic.

Once I ran at a fair in the noise
To catch a greased piglet
That was faster and nimbler than a cat,
Its squeal was the rending of metal.

Pigs must have hot blood, they feel like ovens.
Their bite is worse than a horse's—
They chop a half-moon clean out.
They eat cinders, dead cats.

Distinctions and admirations such
As this one was long finished with.
I stared at it a long time. They were going to scald it,
Scald it and scour it like a doorstep.

In Time of Pestilence, 1593 : *Thomas Nashe*

Adieu, farewell earth's bliss!
This world uncertain is:
Fond are life's lustful joys,
Death proves them all but toys.
None from his darts can fly;
I am sick, I must die—
      Lord, have mercy on us!

Rich men, trust not in wealth,
Gold cannot buy you health;
Physic himself must fade;
All things to end are made;
The plague full swift goes by;
I am sick, I must die—
      Lord, have mercy on us!

Beauty is but a flower
Which wrinkles will devour;
Brightness falls from the air;
Queens have died young and fair;
Dust hath closed Helen's eye;
I am sick, I must die—
      Lord, have mercy on us!

Strength stoops unto the grave,
Worms feed on Hector brave;
Swords may not fight with fate;
Earth still holds ope her gate;
Come, come! the bells do cry;
I am sick, I must die—
      Lord, have mercy on us!

The Main Course

Wit with his wantonness
Tasteth death's bitterness;
Hell's executioner
Hath no ears for to hear
What vain art can reply;
I am sick, I must die —
      Lord, have mercy on us!

Haste therefore each degree
To welcome destiny;
Heaven is our heritage,
Earth but a player's stage.
Mount we unto the sky;
I am sick, I must die —
      Lord, have mercy on us!

Death Fugue : Paul Celan

Black milk of daybreak we drink it at sundown
we drink it at noon in the morning we drink it at night
we drink and we drink it
we dig a grave in the breezes there one lies unconfined
A man lives in the house he plays with the serpents he writes
he writes when dusk falls to Germany your golden hair Margarete
he writes it and steps out of doors and the stars are flashing he
                           whistles his pack out
he whistles his Jews out in earth has them dig for a grave
he commands us strike up for the dance

Black milk of daybreak we drink you at night
we drink in the morning at noon we drink you at sundown
we drink and we drink you
A man lives in the house he plays with the serpents he writes
he writes when dusk falls to Germany your golden hair Margarete
your ashen hair Shulamith we dig a grave in the breezes there one lies
                                   unconfined.

He calls out jab deeper into the earth you lot you others sing now
                                and play
he grabs at the iron in his belt he waves it his eyes are blue
jab deeper you lot with your spades you others play on for the dance

Black milk of daybreak we drink you at night
we drink you at noon in the morning we drink you at sundown

we drink you and we drink you
a man lives in the house your golden hair Margarete
your ashen hair Shulamith he plays with the serpents

He calls out more sweetly play death death is a master from
Germany
he calls out more darkly now stroke your strings then as smoke you
will rise into air
then a grave you will have in the clouds there one lies unconfined

Black milk of daybreak we drink you at night
we drink you at noon death is a master from Germany
we drink you at sundown and in the morning we drink and we drink
you

death is a master from Germany his eyes are blue
he strikes you with leaden bullets his aim is true
a man lives in the house your golden hair Margarete
he sets his pack on to us he grants us a grave in the air
he plays with the serpents and daydreams death is a master from
Germany

your golden hair Margarete
your ashen hair Shulamith

(Translated by Michael Hamburger)

A Hope for those Separated by War :
Sidney Keyes

They crossed her face with blood,
They hung her heart.
They dragged her through a pit
Full of quick sorrow.
Yet her small feet
Ran back on the morrow.

They took his book and caged
His mind in a dark house.
They took his bright eyes
To light their rooms of doubt.
Yet his thin hands
Crawled back and found her out.

The Main Course

Sonnet: "Thou hast made me" : *John Donne*

Thou hast made me, And shall thy worke decay?
Repaire me now, for now mine end doth haste,
I runne to death, and death meets me as fast,
And all my pleasures are like yesterday;
I dare not move my dimme eyes any way,
Despaire behind, and death before doth cast
Such terrour, and my feebled flesh doth waste
By sinne in it, which it t'wards hell doth weigh;
Onely thou art above, and when towards thee
By thy leave I can looke, I rise againe;
But our old subtle foe so tempteth me,
That not one houre my selfe I can sustaine;
Thy Grace may wing me to prevent his art,
And thou like Adamant draw mine iron heart.

Ultima Ratio Regum : *Stephen Spender*

The guns spell money's ultimate reason
In letters of lead on the Spring hillside.
But the boy lying dead under the olive trees
Was too young and too silly
To have been notable to their important eye.
He was a better target for a kiss.

When he lived, tall factory hooters never summoned him
Nor did restaurant plate-glass doors revolve to wave him in
His name never appeared in the papers.
The world maintained its traditional wall
Round the dead with their gold sunk deep as a well,
Whilst his life, intangible as a Stock Exchange rumour, drifted
                                                    outside.

O too lightly he threw down his cap
One day when the breeze threw petals from the trees.
The unflowering wall sprouted with guns,
Machine-gun anger quickly scythed the grasses;
Flags and leaves fell from hands and branches;
The tweed cap rotted in the nettles.

Consider his life which was valueless
In terms of employment, hotel ledgers, news files.
Consider. One bullet in ten thousand kills a man.

Ask. Was so much expenditure justified
On the death of one so young, and so silly
Lying under the olive trees, O world, O death?

Babiy Yar : *Yevgeny Yevtushenko*

Over Babiy Yar
there are no memorials.
The steep hillside like a rough inscription.
I am frightened.
To-day I am as old as the Jewish race.
I seem to myself a Jew at this moment.
I, wandering in Egypt.
I, crucified. I perishing.
Even today the mark of the nails.
I think also of Dreyfus. I am he.
The Philistine my judge and my accuser.
Cut off by bars and cornered,
ringed round, spat at, lied about;
the screaming ladies with the Brussels lace
poke me in the face with parasols.
I am also a boy in Belostok,
the dropping blood spreads across the floor,
the public-bar heroes are rioting
in an equal stench of garlic and of drink.
I have no strength, go spinning from a boot,
shriek useless prayers that they don't listen to;
with a cackle of "Thrash the kikes and save Russia!"
the corn-chandler is beating up my mother.
I seem to myself like Anna Frank
to be transparent as an April twig
and am in love, I have no need for words,
I need for us to look at one another.
How little we have to see or to smell
separated from foliage and the sky,
how much, how much in the dark room
gently embracing each other.
They're coming. Don't be afraid.
The booming and banging of the spring.
It's coming this way. Come to me.
Quickly, give me your lips.
They're battering in the door. Roar of the ice.

Over Babiy Yar
rustle of the wild grass.

The trees look threatening, look like judges.
And everything is one silent cry.
Taking my hat off
I feel myself slowly going grey.
And I am one silent cry
over the many thousands of the buried;
am every old man killed here,
every child killed here.
O my Russian people, I know you.
Your nature is international.
Foul hands rattle your clean name.
I know the goodness of my country.
How horrible it is that pompous title
the anti-semites calmly call themselves,
Society of the Russian Race.
No part of me can ever forget it.
When the last anti-semite on the earth
is buried for ever
let the International ring out.
No Jewish blood runs among my blood,
but I am as bitterly and hardly hated
by every anti-semite
as if I were a Jew. By this
I am a Russian.

(Translated by Robin Milner-Gulland and Peter Levi)

On Wenlock Edge : *A.E.Housman*

On Wenlock Edge the wood's in trouble;
    His forest fleece the Wrekin heaves;
The gale, it plies the saplings double,
    And thick on Severn snow the leaves.

'Twould blow like this through holt and hanger
    When Uricon the city stood:
'Tis the old wind in the old anger,
    But then it threshed another wood.

Then, 'twas before my time, the Roman
    At yonder heaving hill would stare:
The blood that warms an English yeoman,
    The thoughts that hurt him, they were there.

There, like the wind through woods in riot,
    Through him the gale of life blew high;
The tree of man was never quiet:
    Then 'twas the Roman, now 'tis I.

The gale, it plies the saplings double,
    It blows so hard, 'twill soon be gone:
To-day the Roman and his trouble
    Are ashes under Uricon.

Ode. Autumn : *Thomas Hood*

I saw old Autumn in the misty morn
Stand shadowless like Silence, listening
To silence, for no lonely bird would sing
Into his hollow ear from woods forlorn,
Nor lowly hedge nor solitary thorn; —
Shaking his languid locks all dewy bright
With tangled gossamer that fell by night,
    Pearling his coronet of golden corn.

Where are the songs of summer? — With the sun,
Oping the dusky eyelids of the South,
Till shade and silence waken up as one,
And Morning sings with a warm odorous mouth.
Where are the merry birds? — Away, away,
On panting wings through the inclement skies,
      Lest owls should prey
      Undazzled at noonday,
And tear with horny beak their lustrous eyes.

Where are the blooms of Summer? — In the West,
Blushing their last to the last sunny hours,
When the mild Eve by sudden Night is prest
Like tearful Proserpine, snatched from her flowers
      To a most gloomy breast.
Where is the pride of Summer, — the green prime —
The many, many leaves all twinkling? — Three
On the mossed elm; three on the naked lime
Trembling, — and one upon the old oak-tree!
    Where is the Dryad's immortality? —
Gone into mournful cypress and dark yew,
Or wearing the long gloomy Winter through
    In the smooth holly's green eternity.

The Main Course

The squirrel gloats on his accomplished hoard,
The ants have brimmed their garners with ripe grain,
    And honey bees have stored
The sweets of Summer in their luscious cells;
The swallows have all winged across the main;
But here the autumn Melancholy dwells,
And sighs her tearful spells
Amongst the sunless shadows of the plain.
    Alone, alone,
    Upon a mossy stone,
She sits and reckons up the dead and gone
With the last leaves for a love-rosary,
Whilst all the withered world looks drearily,
Like a dim picture of the drowned past
In the hushed mind's mysterious far away,
Doubtful what ghostly thing will steal the last
Into that distance, grey upon the grey.

O go and sit with her, and be o'ershaded
Under the languid downfall of her hair:
She wears a coronal of flowers faded
Upon her forehead, and a face of care; —
There is enough of withered everywhere
To make her bower, — and enough of gloom;
There is enough of sadness to invite,
If only for the rose that died, whose doom
Is Beauty's, — she that with the living bloom
Of conscious cheeks most beautifies the light:
There is enough of sorrowing, and quite
Enough of bitter fruits the earth doth bear, —
Enough of chilly droppings for her bowl;
Enough of fear and shadowy despair,
To frame her cloudy prison for the soul!

Poem in October : *Dylan Thomas*

It was my thirtieth year to heaven
Woke to my hearing from harbour and neighbour wood
And the mussel pooled and the heron
Priested shore
The morning beckon
With water praying and call of seagull and rook
And the knock of sailing boats on the net webbed wall
Myself to set foot
That second
In the still sleeping town and set forth.

My birthday began with the water-
Birds and the birds of the winged trees flying my name
Above the farms and the white horses
And I rose
In rainy autumn
And walked abroad in a shower of all my days.
High tide and the heron dived when I took the road
Over the border
And the gates
Of the town closed as the town awoke.

A springful of larks in a rolling
Cloud and the roadside bushes brimming with whistling
Blackbirds and the sun of October
Summery
On the hill's shoulder,
Here were fond climates and sweet singers suddenly
Come in the morning where I wandered and listened
To the rain wringing
Wind blow cold
In the wood faraway under me.

Pale rain over the dwindling harbour
And over the sea wet church the size of a snail
With its horns through mist and the castle
Brown as owls
But all the gardens
Of spring and summer were blooming in the tall tales
Beyond the border and under the lark full cloud.
There could I marvel
My birthday
Away but the weather turned around.

The Main Course

It turned away from the blithe country
And down the other air and the blue altered sky
Streamed again a wonder of summer
With apples
Pears and red currants
And I saw in the turning so clearly a child's
Forgotten mornings when he walked with his mother
Through the parables
Of sun light
And the legends of the green chapels

And the twice told fields of infancy
That his tears burned my cheeks and his heart moved in mine.
These were the woods the river and sea
Where a boy
In the listening
Summertime of the dead whispered the truth of his joy
To the trees and the stones and the fish in the tide.
And the mystery
Sang alive
Still in the water and singing birds.

And there could I marvel my birthday
Away but the weather turned around. And the true
Joy of the long dead child sang burning
In the sun.
It was my thirtieth
Year to heaven stood there then in the summer noon
Though the town below lay leaved with October blood.
O may my heart's truth
Still be sung
On this high hill in a year's turning.

Field of Autumn : *Laurie Lee*

Slow moves the acid breath of noon
over the copper-coated hill,
slow from the wild crab's bearded breast
the palsied apples fall.

Like coloured smoke the day hangs fire,
taking the village without sound;
the vulture-headed sun lies low
chained to the violet ground.

64

The horse upon the rocky height
rolls all the valley in his eye,
but dares not raise his foot or move
his shoulder from the fly.

The sheep, snail-backed against the wall,
lifts her blind face but does not know
the cry her blackened tongue gives forth
is the first bleat of snow.

Each bird and stone, each roof and well,
feels the gold foot of autumn pass;
each spider binds with glittering snare
the splintered bones of grass.

Slow moves the hour that sucks our life,
slow drops the late wasp from the flower,
the rose tree's thread of scent draws thin —
and snaps upon the air.

Autumn Crocuses : *Guillaume Apollinaire*

The meadow is poisonous but pretty in the autumn
The cows that graze there
Are slowly poisoned
Meadow-saffron the colour of lilac and of shadows
Under the eyes grows there your eyes are like those flowers
Mauve as their shadows and mauve as this autumn
And for your eyes' sake my life is slowly poisoned

Children from school come with their commotion
Dressed in smocks and playing the mouth-organ
Picking autumn crocuses which are like their mothers
Daughters of their daughters and the colour of your eyelids
Which flutter like flowers in the mad breeze blown

The cowherd sings softly to himself all alone
While slowly moving lowing the cows leave behind them
Forever this great meadow ill flowered by the autumn

(Translated by Oliver Bernard)

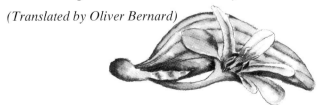

The Main Course

Hunt the thimble : *Dannie Abse*

Hush now. You cannot describe it.

Is it like heavy rain falling,
and lights going on, across the fields,
in the new housing estate?

Cold, cold. Too domestic, too
temperate, too devoid of history.

Is it like a dark windowed street at night,
the houses uncurtained, the street deserted?

Colder. You are getting colder,
and too romantic, too dream-like.
You cannot describe it.

The brooding darkness then,
that breeds inside a cathedral
of a provincial town in Spain?

In Spain, also, but not Spanish.
In England, if you like, but not English.
It remains, even when obscure, perpetually.
Aged, but ageless, you cannot describe it.
No, you are cold, altogether too cold.

Aha—the blue sky over Ampourias,
the blue sky over Lancashire for that matter...

You cannot describe it.

...obscured by clouds?
I must know what you mean.

Hush, hush.

Like those old men in hospital dying,
who, unaware strangers stand around their bed,
stare obscurely, for a long moment,
at one of their own hands raised—
which perhaps is bigger than the moon again—
and then, drowsy, wandering, shout out "Mama".

Is it like that? Or hours after that even:
the darkness inside a dead man's mouth?

No, no, I have told you:
you are cold, and you cannot describe it.

Lord Randal : *Anon*

"O where have you been, Lord Randal, my son?
O where have you been, my handsome young man?" —
    "I have been to the wild wood; mother, make my bed soon,
    For I'm weary with hunting, and fain would lie down."

"Who gave you your dinner, Lord Randal, my son?
Who gave you your dinner, my handsome young man?" —
    "I dined with my sweetheart; mother, make my bed soon,
    For I'm weary with hunting, and fain would lie down."

"What had you for dinner, Lord Randal, my son?
What had you for dinner, my handsome young man?" —
    "I had eels boiled in broth; mother, make my bed soon,
    For I'm weary with hunting, and fain would lie down."

"And where are your bloodhounds, Lord Randal, my son?
And where are your bloodhounds, my handsome young man?" —
    "O they swelled and they died; mother, make my bed soon,
    For I'm weary with hunting, and fain would lie down."

"O I fear you are poisoned, Lord Randal, my son!
O I fear you are poisoned, my handsome young man!" —
    "O yes! I am poisoned; mother, make my bed soon,
    For I'm sick at heart, and I fain would lie down."

The Main Course

Porphyria's Lover : *Robert Browning*

The rain set early in to-night,
    The sullen wind was soon awake,
It tore the elm-tops down for spite,
    And did its worst to vex the lake:
    I listen'd with heart fit to break.
When glided in Porphyria; straight
    She shut the cold out and the storm,
And kneel'd and made the cheerless grate
    Blaze up, and all the cottage warm;
    Which done, she rose, and from her form
Withdrew the dripping cloak and shawl,
    And laid her soil'd gloves by, untied
Her hat and let the damp hair fall,
    And, last, she sat down by my side
    And call'd me. When no voice replied,
She put her arm about my waist,
    And made her smooth white shoulder bare,
And all her yellow hair displaced,
    And, stooping, made my cheek lie there,
    And spread, o'er all, her yellow hair,
Murmuring how she loved me—she
    Too weak, for all her heart's endeavour,
To set its struggling passion free
    From pride, and vainer ties dissever,
    And give herself to me for ever.
But passion sometimes would prevail,
    Nor could to-night's gay feast restrain
A sudden thought of one so pale
    For love of her, and all in vain:
    So, she was come through wind and rain.
Be sure I look'd up at her eyes
    Happy and proud; at last I knew
Porphyria worshipp'd me; surprise
    Made my heart swell, and still it grew
    While I debated what to do.
That moment she was mine, mine, fair,
    Perfectly pure and good: I found
A thing to do, and all her hair
    In one long yellow string I wound
    Three times her little throat around,
And strangled her. No pain felt she;
    I am quite sure she felt no pain.
As a shut bud that holds a bee,

I warily oped her lids; again
    Laugh'd the blue eyes without a stain.
And I untighten'd next the tress
    About her neck; her cheek once more
Blush'd bright beneath my burning kiss:
    I propp'd her head up as before,
    Only, this time my shoulder bore
Her head, which droops upon it still:
    The smiling rosy little head,
So glad it has its utmost will,
    That all it scorn'd at once is fled,
    And I, its love, am gain'd instead!
Porphyria's love: she guess'd not how
    Her darling one wish would be heard.
And thus we sit together now,
    And all night long we have not stirr'd,
    And yet God has not said a word!

A Slumber did my spirit seal :
William Wordsworth

A slumber did my spirit seal:
    I had no human fears:
She seemed a thing that could not feel
    The touch of earthly years.

No motion has she now, no force;
    She neither hears nor sees;
Rolled round in earth's diurnal course,
    With rocks, and stones, and trees.

The Main Course

Fear no more the heat o' the sun :
William Shakespeare

Fear no more the heat o' the sun,
　　Nor the furious winter's rages;
Thou thy worldly task hast done,
　　Home art gone and ta'en thy wages:
Golden lads and girls all must,
As chimney-sweepers come to dust.

Fear no more the frown o' the great;
　　Thou art past the tyrant's stroke;
Care no more to clothe and eat;
　　To thee the reed is as the oak:
The sceptre, learning, physic, must
All follow this and come to dust.

Fear no more the lightning-flash,
　　Nor the all-dreaded thunder-stone;
Fear not slander, censure rash;
　　Thou hast finish'd joy and moan:
All lovers young, all lovers must
Consign to thee and come to dust.

No exorciser harm thee!
Nor no witchcraft charm thee!
Ghost unlaid forbear thee!
Nothing ill come near thee!
Quiet consummation have;
And renownèd be thy name.

Lives : *Henry Reed*

You cannot cage a field.
You cannot wire it, as you wire a summer's roses
To sell in towns; you cannot cage it
Or kill it utterly. All you can do is to force
Year after year from the stream to the cold woods
The heavy glitter of wheat, till its body tires
And the yield grows weaker and dies. But the field never dies,

Though you build on it, burn it black, or domicile
A thousand prisoners upon its empty features.
You cannot kill a field. A field will reach
Right under the streams to touch the limbs of its brothers.

But you can cage the woods.
You can throw up fences, as round a recalcitrant heart
Spring up remonstrances. You can always cage the woods,
Hold them completely. Confine them to hill or valley,
You can alter their face, their shape; uprooting their outer saplings

You can even alter their wants, and their smallest longings
Press to your own desires. The woods succumb
To the paths made through their life, withdraw the trees,
Betake themselves where you tell them, and acquiesce.
The woods retreat; their protest of leaves whirls
Pitifully to the cooling heavens, like dead or dying prayers.

But what can you do with a stream?
You can widen it here, or deepen it there, but even
If you alter its course entirely it gives the impression
That this is what it always wanted. Moorhens return
To nest or hide in the reeds which quickly grow up there,
The fishes breed in it, stone settles on to stone.
The stream announces its places where the water will bubble

Daily and unconcerned, contentedly ruffling and scuffling
With the drifting sky or the leaf. Whatever you do,
A stream has rights, for a stream is always water;
To cross it you have to bridge it; and it will not flow uphill.

On this Island : *W. H. Auden*

Look, stranger, on this island now
The leaping light for your delight discovers,
Stand stable here
And silent be,
That through the channels of the ear
May wander like a river
The swaying sound of the sea.

Here at the small field's ending pause
When the chalk wall falls to the foam and its tall ledges
Oppose the pluck

The Main Course

And knock of the tide,
And the shingle scrambles after the suck-
ing surf,
And the gull lodges
A moment on its sheer side.

Far off like floating seeds the ships
Diverge on urgent voluntary errands,
And the full view
Indeed may enter
And move in memory as now these clouds do,
That pass the harbour mirror
And all the summer through the water saunter.

Home-thoughts from Abroad : *Robert Browning*

Oh, to be in England now that April's there,
And whoever wakes in England sees, some morning, unaware,
That the lowest boughs and the brushwood sheaf
Round the elm-tree bole are in tiny leaf,
While the chaffinch sings on the orchard bough
    In England—now!

    And after April, when May follows,
And the whitethroat builds, and all the swallows!
Hark, where my blossomed pear-tree in the hedge
    Leans to the field and scatters on the clover
Blossoms and dewdrops—at the bent spray's edge—
    That's the wise thrush; he sings each song twice over,
Lest you should think he never could recapture
    The first fine careless rapture!
And though the fields look rough with hoary dew,
All will be gay when noontide wakes anew
The buttercups, the little children's dower
—Far brighter than this gaudy melon-flower!

Kubla Khan : *Samuel Taylor Coleridge*

In Xanadu did Kubla Khan
A stately pleasure-dome decree:
Where Alph, the sacred river, ran
Through caverns measureless to man
    Down to a sunless sea.
So twice five miles of fertile ground
With walls and towers were girdled round:
And there were gardens bright with sinuous rills,
Where blossomed many an incense-bearing tree;
And here were forests ancient as the hills,
Enfolding sunny spots of greenery.

But oh! that deep romantic chasm which slanted
Down the green hill athwart a cedarn cover!
A savage place! as holy and enchanted
As e'er beneath a waning moon was haunted
By woman wailing for her demon-lover!
And from this chasm, with ceaseless turmoil seething,
As if this earth in fast thick pants were breathing,
A mighty fountain momently was forced:
Amid whose swift half-intermitted burst
Huge fragments vaulted like rebounding hail,
Or chaffy grain beneath the thresher's flail:
And 'mid these dancing rocks at once and ever
It flung up momently the sacred river.

Five miles meandering with a mazy motion
Through wood and dale the sacred river ran,
Then reached the caverns measureless to man,
And sank in tumult to a lifeless ocean:
And 'mid this tumult Kubla heard from far
Ancestral voices prophesying war!
    The shadow of the dome of pleasure
    Floated midway on the waves;
    Where was heard the mingled measure
    From the fountain and the caves.
It was a miracle of rare device,
A sunny pleasure-dome with caves of ice!

    A damsel with a dulcimer
    In a vision once I saw:
    It was an Abyssinian maid,
    And on her dulcimer she played,

The Main Course

Singing of Mount Abora.
Could I revive within me
Her symphony and song,
    To such a deep delight 'twould win me,
That with music loud and long,
I would build that dome in air,
That sunny dome! those caves of ice!
And all who heard should see them there,
And all should cry, Beware! Beware!
His flashing eyes, his floating hair!
Wave a circle round him thrice,
And close your eyes with holy dread,
For he on honey-dew hath fed,
And drunk the milk of Paradise.

Chez M. Prieur : *Paul Dehn*

The still rain drops; the raindrops still
Navigate my window-sill,
Where I watched them yesterday;
And still beyond the dripping eaves
By tanglewood and willow-leaves
The river bears the rain away.

From willow-tree to window-pane
Between the river and the rain
The garden's green asylum goes.
Here, the indecent toadstools sprout
And bryony that twists about
The thorny ropes of rambler rose.

Burdock, bindweed, barley-grass,
Razor-blade and broken glass
Constrict the worm that never dies.
Look! where maternal marrows sprawl.
The penitential raindrops fall
From chicory with wet blue eyes.

A flat, black boat, its bloat, fat back
Aground among the garden wrack
Lies where it has always lain,
Though yarrow-foam and sorrel-sand
Weave a slipway overland
To meet the river and the rain.

Though sorrel-sand and yarrow-foam
Call the stranded exile home,
The garden whispers: "Peace! Be still."
And still the river sings beyond
The seven catfish in the pond
Who may not wander where they will.

Another time, another day
(I sit and dream the rain away)
The wind sang, the sun shone.
O visionary weather-vane,
Point the west wind home again
And let the prisoners be gone.

Let convolvulus at dawn
Creep across a ghostly lawn
In flight from the captivity.
Shift the wind, unfix the star
Till the fever-swamps, that are,
Were not and will never be;

Till the boat in sunlight rides
With water slapping both its sides
On a noonday pleasure-cruise,
In the green shadow of whose wake
Voluptuary catfish take
Their dappled ease among the ooze.

Here, beyond my boyhood's eye,
Where salmon-coloured sandbanks lie,
The white birds whistle to the sea;
And fish and boat and bird are one,
Moving seaward in the sun.
O God of Gardens, set them free.

The still rain drops; the raindrops still
Navigate my window-sill,
Where I watched them yesterday;
And still beyond the dripping eaves
By tanglewood and willow-leaves
The river bears the rain away.

The Main Course

A wet sheet and a flowing sea :
Allan Cunningham

A wet sheet and a flowing sea,
    A wind that follows fast
And fills the white and rustling sail
    And bends the gallant mast;
And bends the gallant mast, my boys,
    While like the eagle free
Away the good ship flies, and leaves
    Old England on the lee.

O for a soft and gentle wind!
    I heard a fair one cry;
But give to me the snoring breeze
    And white waves heaving high;
And white waves heaving high, my lads,
    The good ship tight and free —
The world of waters is our home,
    And merry men are we.

There's tempest in yon horned moon,
    And lightning in yon cloud;
But hark the music, mariners!
    The wind is piping loud;
The wind is piping loud, my boys,
    The lightning flashes free —
While the hollow oak our palace is,
    Our heritage the sea.

Beware, good ship : *Horace, Ode IV*

Beware, good ship! Fresh squalls are taking
You out to sea again. Start making
    For harbour, run in hard.
    Listen — a groaning yard;

And look — both sides stripped, oars gone, mast
Crippled by the sou'wester's blast.
    The hull can scarcely hope,
    Shorn of its girding-rope,

To ride the ungovernable seas;
Your sails are torn; the images
 To which, hard pressed, you turn
 Have vanished from the stern.

Daughter you may be of a fine
Plantation, true-bred Pontic pine,
 But pride of name and wood
 Will do you little good.

No sailor puts his trust in mere
Paintwork in danger. Good ship, steer
 Wisely—or on a rock
 Be the wind's laughing-stock.

O once my worry and despair,
But now my loving charge and care,
 Avoid the Cyclades:
 Bright islands, treacherous seas.

(Translated by James Michie)

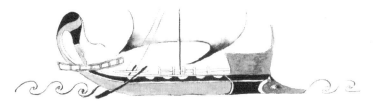

Bermudas : *Andrew Marvell*

Where the remote *Bermudas* ride
In the Ocean's bosom unespied,
From a small boat that rowed along
The listening woods received this song:

 'What should we do but sing His praise
That led us through the watery maze
Unto an isle so long unknown,
And yet far kinder than our own?
Where He the huge sea-monsters wracks,
That lift the deep upon their backs,
He lands us on a grassy stage,
Safe from the storms' and prelates' rage:
He gave us this eternal Spring
Which here enamels everything,

The Main Course

And sends the fowls to us in care
On daily visits through the air:
He hangs in shades the orange bright
Like golden lamps in a green night,
And does in the pomegranates close
Jewels more rich than Ormus shows:
He makes the figs our mouths to meet
And throws the melons at our feet;
But apples plants of such a price,
No tree could ever bear them twice.
With cedars chosen by His hand
From Lebanon he stores the land;
And makes the hollow seas that roar
Proclaim the ambergris on shore.
He cast (of which we rather boast)
The Gospel's pearl upon our coast;
And in these rocks for us did frame
A temple where to sound His name.
O, let our voice His praise exalt
Till it arrive at Heaven's vault,
Which thence (perhaps) rebounding may
Echo beyond the Mexique bay!'

Thus sang they in the English boat
A holy and a cheerful note:
And all the way, to guide their chime,
With falling oars they kept the time.

Lament for the Great Yachts : *Patric Dickinson*

For Tom Rice Henn

Suddenly into my dream why should they come
Closehauled from the west, from Cowes, beating
Out to the Nab with bones in their delicate teeth,
   The old-fashioned beautiful cutters
    The great yachts,
     Bowsprit and topsail, gaff and flying jib:
     Shamrock glittering green;
      Candida, Astra, Lulworth, white; and *Brittania*
   Ebony-black and bronze as she heels hard
When the old King takes the wheel and brings her up
Another two points to the wind and the sea hisses
    And her lee goes flowing under.

And carving the water, saving her time, the *Westward,*
The noblest ever, the perfect racing schooner;
Why should they suddenly steer from the bright blue
   Of a boyhood summer out on the popping seaweed
     And barnacle rocks—
      My naked feet slow-savouring their teeth
      And my gray shorts wet to the thighs—
      I saw them there and loved their ravishing grace
   With a siren's lust, I wanted them to be mine
And I wanted the King to win, always to win
As he did when the wind blew hard and the Ryde steamers
      Were queasy even in Portsmouth with towny trippers.

And I hated the *Lulworth,* she was the ugliest:
And once as the great yachts passed Fort Gilkicker
Out at Spithead, there passed them hurrying inward
   The *Mauretania* the truly most beautiful
    Of steamships ever built—
     Perfection fabulous, never again to be known,
     Never never again,
     And I saw these thoroughbred creatures of seamankind
   Race on the English-summer-coloured-water
Again in a dream, yet human eye shall see them
To the world's end never never again
     In the stiff sou'wester bucking and lively as light.

O and in fact I remember them: thousands must.
But we shall die, and few as lucky as I
Will have a bright dream couple with memory
   In sudden and unpremeditable love—
    May my luck hold!
     For men may explain the logic and dialectic
     That dragged them to the bottom
     To let the silt and slimy water-dust
   Settle upon their pride of wood and metal,
But racing I saw them, darlings of the weather,
Identities of skill, anatomies perfect,
     And now for ever lost for ever lost.

And I have felt their white sails crumple and fall
And the bare masts seem too tall, the hulls riding
Sadly like sleeping bodies, until my spirit
   Blew gale-force and dragged my anchored body
    In never mournful mood,
     But in a joyful agony of acceptance:

The Main Course

As waking I accept the twenty years
That have moved the furniture of my own flesh
From that small room upon a rocky pier
Where I looked out to see my holiday
And wanted it to keep, to keep for ever
Under my pillow like a beloved toy.

And there it lay, to bring after twenty years
An absolute joy, a strange and marvellous thing:
How little it is I can pass on or share!
They had their Royal week of Cowes Regatta,
Fireworks and flags
And ships like jewellers cutting the precious sea.
But my words are neither Solent winds nor tides,
They are things forgotten, sentimental chimes,
Bowsprit and topsail, gaff and flying jib.
Their meanings wash against this later day
Rubbing the names off: *Astra, Candida,*
Shamrock, Westward, Lulworth, Brittania.

Gloucester Moors : *William Vaughn Moody*

A mile behind is Gloucester town
Where the fishing fleets put in,
A mile ahead the land dips down
And the woods and farms begin.
Here, where the moors stretch free
In the high blue afternoon,
Are the marching sun and talking sea,
And the racing winds that wheel and flee
On the flying heels of June.

Jill-o'er-the-ground is purple blue,
Blue is the quaker-maid,
The wild geranium holds its dew
Long in the boulder's shade.
Wax-red hangs the cup
From the huckleberry boughs,
In barberry bells the grey moths sup,
Or where the choke-cherry lifts high up
Sweet bowls for their carouse.

Over the shelf of the sandy cove
Beach-peas blossom late.
By copse and cliff the swallows rove
Each calling to his mate.
Seaward the sea-gulls go,
And the land-birds all are here;
That green-gold flash was a vireo,
And yonder flame where the marsh-flags grow
Was a scarlet tanager.

This earth is not the steadfast place
We landsmen build upon;
From deep to deep she varies pace,
And while she comes is gone.
Beneath my feet I feel
Her smooth bulk heave and dip;
With velvet plunge and soft upreel
She swings and steadies to her keel
Like a gallant, gallant ship.

These summer clouds she sets for sail,
The sun is her masthead light,
She tows the moon like a pinnace frail
Where her phosphor wake churns bright.

The Main Course

Now hid, now looming clear,
On the face of the dangerous blue
The star fleets tack and wheel and veer,
But on, but on does the old earth steer
As if her port she knew.

God, dear God! Does she know her port,
Though she goes so far about?
Or blind astray, does she make her sport
To brazen and chance it out?
I watched when her captains passed:
She were better captainless.
Men in the cabin, before the mast,
But some were reckless and some aghast,
And some sat gorged at mess.

By her battened hatch I leaned and caught
Sounds from the noisome hold, —
Cursing and sighing of souls distraught
And cries too sad to be told.
Then I strove to go down and see;
But they said, "Thou art not of us!"
I turned to those on the deck with me
And cried, "Give help!" But they said, "Let be:
Our ship sails faster thus."

Jill-o'er-the-ground is purple blue,
Blue is the quaker-maid,
The alder-clump where the brook comes through
Breeds cresses in its shade.
To be out of the moiling street
With its swelter and its sin!
Who has given to me this sweet,
And given my brother dust to eat?
And when will his wage come in?

Scattering wide or blown in ranks,
Yellow and white and brown,
Boats and boats from the fishing banks
Come home to Gloucester town.
There is cash to purse and spend,
There are wives to be embraced,
Hearts to borrow and hearts to lend,
And hearts to take and keep to the end, —
O little sails, make haste!

But thou, vast outbound ship of souls,
What harbor town for thee?
What shapes, when thy arriving tolls,
Shall crowd the banks to see?
Shall all the happy shipmates then
Stand singing brotherly?
Or shall a haggard ruthless few
Warp her over and bring her to,
While the many broken souls of men
Fester down in the slaver's pen,
And nothing to say or do?

At Porthcothan : *Christopher Middleton*

A speck of dark at low tide on the tideline,
It could not be identified as any known thing,
Until, as one approached, a neck was clear
(It is agreed that logs, or cans, are neckless),
And then a body, over which the neck stood
Curved like a questionmark, emerged
As oval, and the whole shape was crouching
Helpless in a small pool the sea had left.

The oval body, with green sheen as of pollen
Shading off into the black plumage, and the neck
Surmounted by the tiny wide-eyed head,
Were not without beauty. The head was moving,
So like a cobra it seemed rash to offer
An introductory finger to the long hooked bill
Stabbing the air. Danger had so
Sharpened what intelligence the bird possessed,
It seemed to pierce the mind of the observer.
In fact we were afraid, yes afraid of each other.

Finally though I picked it up and took it
To a quiet side-bay where dogs were rarer.
Here the shag sat, happy in the sun,
Perched on a slab of rock where a pool was,
In which I caught five fish for it
With a pocketknife, a handkerchief
And a plunging forefinger. But at six o'clock
It left the rock and waddled off seaward.

The Main Course

Though breakers came in high and curling
It straddled them, bouncing, buoyant,
Borne along the sealine sideways, with head up,
Slithering across the bay's whole width, and then
Drifted ashore again, to scuttle flapping
With webbed feet flat like a Saturday banker's
To shelter on a level rock. Here it studied,
With the air of one of whom something is expected,
The turbulent Atlantic slowly rising.
What could I do but leave it meditating?

Early next morning, on the bay's north side,
I found it cuddled under the cliff. The tide
Was low again. What hungry darkness
Had driven so the dark young shag to shelter?
It did not resist when I picked it up.
Something had squeezed the cobra out of it.

I took it to a cave where the sun shone in,
Then caught two fish. It opened one green eye,
And then another. But though I cut
The fish into portions, presenting these
To the bill's hooked tip, it only shook its head.
Noon came. The shag slept in the cave. At two
I hurried back. The shag was stone dead,
With its fine glossy head laid back a little
Over the left shoulder, and a few flies
Were pestering its throat and the fish scraps
Now unlikely to get eaten.

       Ten minutes perhaps
I sat there, then carried it up the cliff path

And across the headland to a neighbouring cove
Where oystercatchers and hawks flew and far
Far below in loose heaps small timber lay, tickled
By a thin finger of sea. There I flung down the shag,
For in some such place, I thought,
Such bodies best belong, far from bathers, among
The elements that compose and decompose them,
Unconscious, strange to freedom, but perceptible
Through narrow slits that score the skin of things.

Or perhaps (for I could not see the body falling)
A hand rose out of air and plucked the corpse
From its arc and took it, warm still,
To some safer place and concealed it there,
Quite unobtrusively, but sure, but sure.

Sea Love : *Charlotte Mew*

Tide be runnin' the great world over:
    'Twas only last June month I mind that we
Was thinkin' the toss and the call in the breast of the lover
    So everlastin' as the sea.

Heer's the same little fishes that sputter and swim,
    Wi' the moon's old glim on the grey, wet sand;
An' him no more to me nor me to him
    Than the wind goin' over my hand.

The Tide rises, the Tide falls : *Henry Wadsworth Longfellow*

The tide rises, the tide falls,
The twilight darkens, the curlew calls;
Along the sea-sands damp and brown
The traveller hastens towards the town,
    And the tide rises, the tide falls.

Darkness settles on roofs and walls,
But the sea, the sea in the darkness calls;
The little waves with their soft, white hands,
Efface the footprints in the sands,
    And the tide rises, the tide falls.

The Main Course

The morning breaks; the steeds in their stalls
Stamp and neigh, as the hostler calls;
The day returns, but nevermore
Returns the traveller to the shore,
    And the tide rises, the tide falls.

Magna est Veritas : *Coventry Patmore*

Here, in this little Bay,
Full of tumultuous life and great repose,
Where, twice a day,
The purposeless, glad ocean comes and goes,
Under high cliffs, and far from the huge town,
I sit me down.
For want of me the world's course will not fail:
When all its work is done, the lie shall rot;
The truth is great, and shall prevail,
When none cares whether it prevail or not.

Conversation
between Courses

Ancient Music : *Ezra Pound*

Winter is icummen in
Llude sing Goddamm,
Raineth drop and staineth slop,
And how the wind doth ramm!
            Sing: Goddamm.
Skiddeth bus and sloppeth us,
An ague hath my ham.
Freezeth river, turneth liver,
            Damn you, sing: Goddamm.
Goddamm, Goddamm, 'tis why I am, Goddamm,
            So 'gainst the winter's balm.
Sing goddamm, damm, sing Goddamm,
Sing goddamm, sing goddamm, DAMM.

A Parental Ode to my Son, aged three years and five months : *Thomas Hood*

    Thou happy, happy elf!
(But stop—first let me kiss away that tear)—
    Thou tiny image of myself!
(My love, he's poking peas into his ear!)
Thou merry, laughing sprite!
With spirits feather-light,
Untouched by sorrow, and unsoiled by sin—
(Good heavens! the child is swallowing a pin!)

    Thou little tricky Puck!
With antic toys so funnily bestuck,
Light as the singing bird that wings the air—
(The door! the door! he'll tumble down the stair!)
    Thou darling of thy sire!
(Why, Jane, he'll set his pinafore a-fire!)
    Thou imp of mirth and joy!
In love's dear chain so strong and bright a link,
Thou idol of thy parents—(drat the boy!
       there goes my ink!)

    Thou cherub—but of earth;
Fit playfellow for Fays by moonlight pale,
    In harmless sport and mirth,
(That dog will bite him if he pulls its tail!)

Conversation between Courses

Thou human humming-bee, extracting honey
From every blossom in the world that blows,
    Singing in Youth's Elysium ever sunny—
    (Another tumble!—that's his precious nose!)

    Thy father's pride and hope!
(He'll break the mirror with that skipping-rope!)
With pure heart newly stamped from nature's mint,
    (Where *did* he learn that squint?)
    Thou young domestic dove!
(He'll have that jug off, with another shove!)
    Dear nursling of the hymeneal nest!
    (Are those torn clothes his best?)
    Little epitome of man!
(He'll climb upon the table, that's his plan!)
Touched with the beauteous tints of dawning life,
      (He's got a knife!)

    Thou enviable being!
No storms, no clouds, in the blue sky foreseeing,
    Play on, play on,
    My elfin John!
Toss the light ball—bestride the stick—
(I knew so many cakes would make him sick!)
With fancies buoyant as the thistledown,
Prompting the face grotesque, and antic brisk,
    With many a lamb-like frisk—
(He's got the scissors, snipping at your gown!)

    Thou pretty opening rose!
(Go to your mother, child, and wipe your nose!)
Balmy, and breathing music like the South,
(He really brings my heart into my mouth!)
Fresh as the morn, and brilliant as its star—
(I wish that window had an iron bar!)
Bold as a hawk, yet gentle as the dove—
    (I'll tell you what, my love,
I cannot write unless he's sent above!)

Speak roughly to your little boy : *Lewis Carroll*

Speak roughly to your little boy,
    And beat him when he sneezes;
He only does it to annoy,
    Because he knows it teases.
        Chorus: Wow! Wow! Wow!

I speak severely to my boy,
    I beat him when he sneezes;
For he can thoroughly enjoy
    The pepper when he pleases!
        Chorus: Wow! Wow! Wow!

A Glass of Beer : *James Stephens*

The lanky hank of a she in the inn over there
Nearly killed me for asking the loan of a glass of beer:
May the devil grip the whey-faced slut by the hair,
And beat bad manners out of her for a year.

That parboiled imp, with the hardest jaw you will see
On virtue's path, and a voice that would rasp the dead,
Came roaring and raging the minute she looked at me,
And threw me out of the house on the back of my head!

If I asked her master he'd give me a cask a day;
But she with the beer at hand, not a gill would arrange!
May she marry a ghost and bear him a kitten and may
The High King of Glory permit her to get the mange.

In Defence of Drunkards : *Jan Kochanowski*

Earth, that drinks rain, refreshes the trees:
Oceans drink rivers: stars quaff up the seas:
So why should they make such a terrible fuss
Over insignificant tipplers like us?

(Translated by Jerzy Peterkiewicz and Burns Singer)

Conversation between Courses

To Be or Not To Be : *Anon*

I sometimes think I'd rather crow
And be a rooster than to roost
And be a crow. But I dunno.

A rooster he can roost also,
Which don't seem fair when crows can't crow.
Which may help some. Still I dunno.

Crows should be glad of one thing, though;
Nobody thinks of eating crow,
While roosters they are good enough
For anyone unless they're tough.

There are lots of tough old roosters though,
And anyway a crow can't crow,
So mebby roosters stand more show.
It looks that way. But I don't know.

When the frost is on the punkin : *James Whitcomb Riley*

When the frost is on the punkin and the fodder's in the shock,
And you hear the kyouck and gobble of the struttin' turkey-cock,
And the clackin' of the guineys, and the cluckin' of the hens,
And the rooster's hallylooyer as he tiptoes on the fence;
O, it's then's the times a feller is a-feelin' at his best,
With the risin' sun to greet him from a night of peaceful rest,
As he leaves the house, bareheaded, and goes out to feed the stock,
When the frost is on the punkin and the fodder's in the shock.

They's something kindo' harty-like about the atmusfere
When the heat of summer's over and the coolin' fall is here —
Of course we miss the flowers, and the blossums on the trees,
And the mumble of the hummin'-birds and buzzin' of the bees;
But the air's so appetizin'; and the landscape through the haze
Of a crisp and sunny morning of the airly autumn days
Is a pictur' that no painter has the colorin' to mock —
When the frost is on the punkin and the fodder's in the shock.

The husky, rusty russel of the tossels of the corn,
And the raspin' of the tangled leaves, as golden as the morn;
The stubble in the furries — kindo' lonesome-like, but still

A-preachin' sermuns to us of the barns they growed to fill;
The strawstack in the medder, and the reaper in the shed;
The hosses in theyr stalls below—the clover overhead!—
O, it sets my hart a-clickin' like the tickin' of a clock,
When the frost is on the punkin and the fodder's in the shock!

Then your apples all is getherd, and the ones a feller keeps
Is poured around the celler-floor in red and yeller heaps;
And your cider-makin's over, and your wimmern-folks is through
With theyr mince and apple-butter, and theyr souse and sausage,
too!...

I don't know how to tell it—but ef sich a thing could be
As the Angels wantin' boardin', and they'd call around on *me*—
I'd want to 'commodate 'em—all the whole-indurin' flock—
When the frost is on the punkin and the fodder's in the shock!

Sensitive, Seldom and Sad : *Mervyn Peake*

Sensitive, Seldom and Sad are we,
As we wend our way to the sneezing sea,
With our hampers full of thistles and fronds
To plant round the edge of the dab-fish ponds;
Oh, so Sensitive, Seldom and Sad—
Oh, *so* Seldom and Sad.

In the shambling shades of the shelving shore,
We will sing us a song of the Long Before,
And light a red fire and warm our paws
For it's chilly, it is, on the Desolate shores,
For those who are Sensitive, Seldom and Sad,
For those who are Seldom and Sad.

Sensitive, Seldom and Sad are we,
As we wander along through Lands Afar,
To the sneezing sea, where the sea-weeds be,
And the dab-fish ponds that are waiting for we
Who are, Oh, so Sensitive, Seldom and Sad,
Oh, *so* Seldom and Sad.

Conversation between Courses

When famed King Arthur ruled this land : *Nursery Rhyme*

When famed King Arthur ruled this land
    He was a goodly king:
He took three pecks of barley meal
    To make a bag pudding.

A rare pudding the king did make,
    And stuffed it well with plums;
And in it put such lumps of fat,
    As big as my two thumbs.

The king and queen did eat thereof,
    And noblemen beside,
And what they could not eat that night
    The queen next morning fried.

Herring is King : *Alfred Perceval Graves*

Let all the fish that swim the sea,
    Salmon and turbot, cod and ling,
Bow down the head and bend the knee
    To herring, their king—to herring, their king!
        Sing, *Thugamar féin an samhradh linn,*
        'Tis we have brought the summer in.

The sun sank down, so round and red,
    Upon the bay, upon the bay;
The sails shook idly overhead—
    Becalmed we lay, becalmed we lay.
        Sing, *Thugamar féin an samhradh linn,*
        'Tis we have brought the summer in.

Till Shawn the eagle dropped on deck,
    The bright-eyed boy, the bright-eyed boy;
'Tis he has spied your silver track,
    Herring, our joy—herring, our joy.
        Sing, *Thugamar féin an samhradh linn,*
        'Tis we have brought the summer in.

It was in with the sails and away to shore,
    With the rise and swing, the rise and swing
Of two stout lads at each smoking oar,

After herring, our king—herring, our king.
    Sing, *Thugamar féin an samhradh linn,*
    'Tis we have brought the summer in.

The Manx and the Cornish raised the shout,
    And joined the chase, and joined the chase,
But their fleets they fouled as they went about,
    And we won the race, we won the race.
    Sing, *Thugamar féin an samhradh linn,*
    'Tis we have brought the summer in.

For we turned and faced you full to land,
    Down the goleen* long, the goleen long,
And after you slipped from strand to strand
    Our nets so strong, our nets so strong.
    Sing, *Thugamar féin an samhradh linn,*
    'Tis we have brought the summer in.

Then we called to our sweethearts and our wives,
    'Come, welcome us home—welcome us home'
Till they ran to meet us for their lives
    Into the foam, into the foam.
    Sing, *Thugamar féin an samhradh linn,*
    'Tis we have brought the summer in.

Oh, the kissing of hands and waving of caps
    From girl and boy, from girl and boy,
While you leapt by scores in the lasses' laps,
    Herring, our joy—herring, our joy.
    Sing, *Thugamar féin an samhradh linn,*
    'Tis we have brought the summer in.

(Line two of the refrain is a translation of the first, pronounced:
Hagamar, fain an sowra linn
*goleen—creek)

The Red Herring : *George MacBeth*

There was once a high wall, a bare wall. And
against this wall, there was a ladder,
a long ladder. And on the ground,
under the ladder, there was a red
herring. A dry red herring.

Conversation between Courses

And then a man came along. And in his hands
(they were dirty hands) this man had
a heavy hammer, a long nail
(it was also a sharp nail) and
a ball of string. A thick ball of string.

All right. So the man climbed up
the ladder (right up to the top)
and knocked in the sharp nail:
spluk! Just like that.
Right on top of the wall. The bare wall.

Then he dropped the hammer. It dropped
right down to the ground. And onto the nail
he tied a piece of string, a long
piece of string, and onto the string,
he tied the red herring. The dry red herring.

And let it drop. And then he climbed
down the ladder (right down
to the bottom), picked up the hammer
and also the ladder (which was pretty heavy)
and went off. A long way off.

And since then, that red herring, the dry
red herring on the end of the string, which is
quite a long piece, has been
very very slowly swinging and
swinging to a stop. A full stop.

I expect you wonder why I made
up this story, such a simple story. Well,
I did it just to annoy people.
Serious people. And perhaps also
to amuse children. Small children.

The Herring : *Walter Scott*

The Herring he loves the merry moonlight
    And the Mackerel loves the wind,
But the Oyster loves the dredging song
    For he comes of a gentler kind.

It Makes a Change : *Mervyn Peake*

There's nothing makes a Greenland Whale
    Feel half so high-and-mighty,
As sitting on a mantelpiece
    In Aunty Mabel's nighty.

It makes a change from Freezing Seas,
    (Of which a Whale can tire),
To warm his weary tail at ease
    Before an English fire.

For this delight he leaves the sea,
    (Unknown to Aunty Mabel),
Returning only when the dawn
    Lights up the breakfast table.

On a Favourite Cat Drowned in a Tub of Goldfishes : *Thomas Gray*

'Twas on a lofty vase's side,
Where China's gayest art had dyed
    The azure flowers that blow;
Demurest of the tabby kind,
The pensive Selima reclined,
    Gazed on the lake below.

Her conscious tail her joy declared;
The fair round face, the snowy beard,
    The velvet of her paws,
Her coat, that with the tortoise vies,
Her ears of jet, and emerald eyes,
    She saw; and purr'd applause.

Still had she gazed; but 'midst the tide
Two angel forms were seen to glide,
    The Genii of the stream:
Their scaly armour's Tyrian hue
Thro' richest purple to the view
    Betray'd a golden gleam.

The hapless Nymph with wonder saw:
A whisker first and then a claw,
    With many an ardent wish,

Conversation between Courses

She stretch'd in vain to reach the prize.
What female heart can gold despise?
    What Cat's averse to fish?

Presumptuous Maid! with looks intent
Again she stretch'd, again she bent,
    Nor knew the gulf between.
(Malignant Fate sat by, and smiled.)
The slipp'ry verge her feet beguiled,
    She tumbled headlong in.

Eight times emerging from the flood
She mew'd to ev'ry wat'ry god,
    Some speedy aid to send.
No Dolphin came, no Nereid stirr'd:
Nor cruel *Tom,* nor *Susan* heard.
    A Fav'rite has no friend!

From hence, ye Beauties undeceived,
Know, one false step is ne'er retrieved,
    And be with caution bold.
Not all that tempts your wand'ring eyes
And heedless hearts, is lawful prize;
    Nor all that glisters, gold.

Beethoven : *John Todhunter*

Music as of the winds when they awake,
    Wailing, in the mid forest; music that raves
    Like moonless tides about forlorn sea-caves
On desolate shores, where swell weird songs and break
In peals of demon laughter; chords athirst
    With restless anguish of divine desires—
    The voice of a vexed soul ere it aspires
With a great cry for light; anon a burst
Of passionate joy—fierce joy of conscious might,
    Down-sinking in voluptuous luxury;
Rich harmonies, full-pulsed with deep delight,
    And melodies dying deliciously
As odorous sighs breathed through the quiet night
    By violets. Thus Beethoven speaks for me.

Free Thoughts on Several Eminent Composers : *Charles Lamb*

Some cry up Haydn, some Mozart,
Just as the whim bites; for my part,
I do not care a farthing candle
For either of them, or for Handel.
Cannot a man live free and easy
Without admiring Pergolesi?
Or through the world with comfort go
That never heard of Doctor Blow?
So help me Heaven, I hardly have;
And yet I eat, and drink, and shave,
Like other people, if you watch it,
And know no more of stave or crotchet
Than did the primitive Peruvians;
Or those old ante-queer-diluvians
That lived in the unwashed world with Jubal,
Before that dirty blacksmith Tubal,
By stroke on anvil, or by summat,
Found out, to his great surprise, the gamut.
I care no more for Cimarosa
Than he did for Salvator Rosa,
Being no painter; and bad luck
Be mine, if I can bear that Gluck!

Old Tycho Brahe and modern Herschel
Had something in them; but who's Purcell?
The devil, with his foot so cloven,
For aught I care, may take Beethoven;
And, if the bargain does not suit,
I'll throw him Weber in to boot!
There's not the splitting of a splinter
To choose 'twixt him last named, and Winter.
Of Doctor Pepusch old Queen Dido
Knew just as much, God knows, as I do.
I would not go four miles to visit
Sebastian Bach (or Batch, which is it?)
No more I would for Bononcini.
As for Novello, or Rossini,
I shall not say a word to grieve 'em,
Because they're living; so I leave 'em.

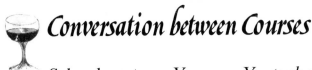

Conversation between Courses

Schoolmaster : *Yevgeny Yevtushenko*

The window gives onto the white trees.
The master looks out of it at the trees,
for a long time, he looks for a long time
out through the window at the trees,
breaking his chalk slowly in one hand.
And it's only the rules of long division.
And he's forgotten the rules of long division.
Imagine not remembering long division!
A mistake on the blackboard, a mistake.
We watch him with a different attention
needing no one to hint to us about it,
there's more than difference in this attention.
The schoolmaster's wife has gone away,
we do not know where she has gone to,
we do not know why she has gone,
what we know is his wife has gone away.

His clothes are neither new nor in the fashion;
wearing the suit he always wears
and which is neither new nor in the fashion
the master goes downstairs to the cloakroom.
He fumbles in his pocket for a ticket.
"What's the matter? Where is that ticket?
Perhaps I never picked up my ticket.
Where is the thing?" Rubbing his forehead.
"Oh, here it is. I'm getting old.
Don't argue auntie dear, I'm getting old.
You can't do much about getting old."
We hear the door below creaking behind him.

The window gives onto the white trees.
The trees are high and wonderful,
but they are not why we are looking out.
We look in silence at the schoolmaster.
He has a bent back and a clumsy walk,
he moves without defences, clumsily,
worn out I ought to have said, clumsily.
Snow falling on him softly through the silence
turns him to white under the white trees.
He whitens into white like the trees.
A little longer will make him so white
we shall not see him in the whitened trees.

(Translated by Robin Milner-Gulland and Peter Levi)

The Two Old Bachelors : *Edward Lear*

Two old Bachelors were living in one house;
One caught a Muffin, the other caught a Mouse.
Said he who caught the Muffin to him who caught the Mouse,—
"This happens just in time! For we've nothing in the house,
Save a tiny slice of lemon and a teaspoonful of honey,
And what to do for dinner—since we haven't any money?
And what can we expect if we haven't any dinner,
But to lose our teeth and eyelashes and keep on growing thinner?"

Said he who caught the Mouse to him who caught the Muffin,—
"We might cook this little Mouse, if we only had some Stuffin'!
If we had but Sage and Onion we could do extremely well,
But how to get that Stuffin' it is difficult to tell"—

Those two old Bachelors ran quickly to the town
And asked for Sage and Onions as they wandered up and down;
They borrowed two large Onions, but no Sage was to be found
In the Shops, or in the Market, or in all the Gardens round.

But some one said,—"A hill there is, a little to the north,
And to its purpledicular top a narrow way leads forth;—
And there among the rugged rocks abides an ancient Sage,—
An earnest Man, who reads all day a most perplexing page.
Climb up, and seize him by the toes!—all studious as he sits,—
And pull him down,—and chop him into endless little bits!
Then mix him with your Onion, (cut up likewise into Scraps,)—
When your Stuffin' will be ready—and very good: perhaps."

Those two old Bachelors without loss of time
the nearly purpledicular crags at once began to climb;
And at the top, among the rocks, all seated in a nook,
They saw that Sage, a-reading of a most enormous book.

"You earnest Sage!" aloud they cried, "your book you've read
enough in!—
We wish to chop you into bits to mix you into Stuffin'!"—

But that old Sage looked calmly up, and with his awful book,
At those two Bachelors' bald heads a certain aim he took;—
And over Crag and precipice they rolled promiscuous down,—
At once they rolled, and never stopped in lane or field or town,—

Conversation between Courses

And when they reached their house, they found (besides their want of Stuffin',)
The Mouse had fled;—and, previously, had eaten up the Muffin.

They left their home in silence by the once convivial door.
And from that hour those Bachelors were never heard of more.

To Heaven by Bus : *Hardiman Scott*

I dreamt I was on my way to heaven,
not in my car, but in a London bus.
The conductor, schooled by Flanders and Swann,
was shouting: "Hold very tight, please"; and that
was surprising, since the bus was not full
and no one was standing. Perhaps he meant
that bewildering collection of thoughts
and things that ornament a life and that
you cling to for security; perhaps
he was thinking of those ragged beliefs
that make do and hang in life like tattered
flags in churches, and there's no certainty
about the victories they represent.
Or maybe he was referring to faith.
I haven't any of that to hold tight.
Come to think of it, he asked for no fare.

I don't remember much of the journey.
There were no other passengers I knew.
I don't suppose I would have known heaven
but for seeing you, my father, smiling
just as I remember you—which itself
prompts questions about ageing, and whether
paradise is an aspic which preserves
the best recollection of a person.
You resisted saying: "I told you so".
That was generous, or it would have been
if this were not a dream; but before we
could discuss the meaning of this meeting,
or mark the nature of reality,
even dispose of the problem of death,
I woke up, feeling hot, needing a pee.

If dreams have meaning, then I'd advise: think
before boarding a London Transport bus.

Afters

A Ternarie of Littles, upon a Pipkin of Jelly sent to a Lady : *Robert Herrick*

A little Saint best fits a little Shrine,
A little Prop best fits a little Vine,
As my small Cruse best fits my little Wine.

A little Seed best fits a little Soil,
A little Trade best fits a little Toil:
As my small Jar best fits my little Oil.

A little Bin best fits a little Bread,
A little Garland fits a little Head;
As my small stuff best fits my little Shed.

A little Hearth best fits a little Fire,
A little Chapel fits a little Choir,
As my small Bell best fits my little Spire.

A little Stream best fits a little Boat,
A little Lead best fits a little Float,
As my small Pipe best fits my little Note.

A little Meat befits a little Belly,
As sweetly, Lady, give me leave to tell'ee,
This little Pipkin fits this little Jelly.

Moonlit Apples : *John Drinkwater*

At the top of the house the apples are laid in rows,
And the skylight lets the moonlight in, and those
Apples are deep-sea apples of green. There goes
    A cloud on the moon in the autumn night.

A mouse in the wainscot scratches, and scratches, and then
There is no sound at the top of the house of men
Or mice; and the cloud is blown, and the moon again
    Dapples the apples with deep-sea light.

They are lying in rows there, under the gloomy beams;
On the sagging floor; they gather the silver streams
Out of the moon, those moonlit apples of dreams,
    And quiet is the steep stair under.

Afters

In the corridors under there is nothing but sleep.
And stiller than ever on orchard boughs they keep
Tryst with the moon, and deep is the silence, deep
    On moon-washed apples of wonder.

August Weather : *Katharine Tynan-Hinkson*

Dead heat and windless air,
    And silence over all;
Never a leaf astir,
    But the ripe apples fall;
Plums are purple-red,
    Pears amber and brown;
Thud! in the garden-bed
    Ripe apples fall down.

Air like a cider-press
    With the bruised apples' scent;
Low whistles express
    Some sleepy bird's content;
Still world and windless sky,
    A mist of heat o'er all;
Peace like a lullaby,
    And the ripe apples fall.

Summer in Spring : *Arthur Symons*

When summer, come before its hour,
With heady draughts of ripe July,
Drugs the wild April, young in flower,
And suns reel drunken in the sky;

These lovely useless London days
In which the sunshine, warm in vain,
Is thickened into hateful haze
Or spilt upon the streets, like rain:

To think how, far on fields of green,
The winds are happy in the grass,
And the first bees begin to glean
The honey of the hours that pass!

Honey Harvest : *Martin Armstrong*

Late in March, when the days are growing longer
    And sight of early green
Tells of the coming spring and suns grow stronger,
Round the pale willow-catkins there are seen
    The year's first honey-bees
Stealing the nectar : and bee-masters know
This for the first sign of the honey-flow.

Then in the dark hillsides the Cherry-trees
Gleam white with loads of blossom where the gleams
Of piled snow lately hung, and richer streams
The honey. Now, if chilly April days
Delay the Apple-blossom, and the May's
First week come, in with sudden summer weather,
The Apple and the Hawthorn bloom together,
And all day long the plundering hordes go round
And every overweighted blossom nods.
But from that gathered essence they compound
Honey more sweet than nectar of the gods.

Those blossoms fall ere June, warm June that brings
The small white Clover. Field by scented field,
Round farms like islands in the rolling weald,
It spreads thick-flowering or in wildness springs
Short-stemmed upon the naked downs, to yield
A richer store of honey than the Rose,
The Pink, the Honeysuckle. Thence there flows
Nectar of clearest amber, redolent
    Of every flowery scent
That the warm wind upgathers as he goes.

In mid-July be ready for the noise
Of million bees in old Lime-avenues,
As though hot noon had found a droning voice
To ease her soul. Here for those busy crews
Green leaves and pale-stemmed clusters of green flowers
Build heavy-perfumed, cool, green-twilight bowers
Whence, load by load, through the long summer days
    They fill their glassy cells
With dark green honey, clear as chrysoprase,
Which housewives shun; but the bee-master tells
This brand is more delicious than all else.

Afters

In August-time, if moors are near at hand,
Be wise and in the evening-twilight load
Your hives upon a cart, and take the road
By night: that, ere the early dawn shall spring
And all the hills turn rosy with the Ling,
    Each waking hive may stand
Established in its new-appointed land
Without harm taken, and the earliest flights
Set out at once to loot the heathery heights.

That vintage of the Heather yields so dense
And glutinous a syrup that it foils
Him who would spare the comb and drain from thence
    Its dark, full-flavoured spoils:
For he must squeeze to wreck the beautiful
Frail edifice. Not otherwise he sacks
Those many-chambered palaces of wax.

Then let a choice of every kind be made,
And, labelled, set upon your storehouse racks—
Of Hawthorn-honey that of almond smacks:
The luscious Lime-tree-honey, green as jade:
Pale Willow-honey, hived by the first rover:
    That delicate honey culled
From Apple-blossom, that of sunlight tastes:
And sunlight-coloured honey of the Clover.
    Then, when the late year wastes,
When night falls early and the noon is dulled
    And the last warm days are over,
Unlock the store and to your table bring
Essence of every blossom of the spring.
And if, when wind has never ceased to blow
All night, you wake to roofs and trees becalmed
    In level wastes of snow,
Bring out the Lime-tree-honey, the embalmed
Soul of a lost July, or Heather-spiced
Brown-gleaming comb wherein sleeps crystallised
All the hot perfume of the heathery slope.
And, tasting and remembering, live in hope.

Sing a Song of Honey : *Barbara Euphan Todd*

Honey from the white rose, honey from the red,
Is not that a pretty thing to spread upon your bread?
When the flower is open, the bee begins to buzz,
I'm very glad, I'm very glad, I'm very glad it does—
Honey from the lily,
    Honey from the May,
AND the daffodilly,
    AND the lilac spray—
When the snow is falling, when the fires are red,
Is that not a pretty thing to spread upon your bread?

Honey from the heather, honey from the lime,
Is not that a dainty thing to eat in winter-time?
Honey from the cherry, honey from the ling,
Honey from the celandine that opens in the spring.
Honey from the clover,
    Honey from the pear—
Summer may be over,
    But I shall never care.
When the fires are blazing, honey from the lime
Makes a very dainty dish to eat in winter time.

Kings will leave their counting any time they're told
Queens are in the parlour spreading honey gold,
Gold from honeysuckle, gold from lupin's spire—
Who will stay in counting-house and miss the parlour fire?
Honey from the daisy,
    Honey from the plum,
Kings will all be lazy,
    And glad that Winter's come.
Who will keep to counting till the sum is told?
I'll be in the parlour and eating honey-gold.

The Wild Honey Suckle : *Philip Freneau*

Fair flower, that dost so comely grow,
Hid in this silent, dull retreat,
Untouched thy honied blossoms blow,
Unseen thy little branches greet:
    No roving foot shall crush thee here,
    No busy hand provoke a tear.

Afters

By Nature's self in white arrayed,
She bade thee shun the vulgar eye,
And planted here the guardian shade,
And sent soft waters murmuring by;
    Thus quietly thy summer goes,
    Thy days declining to repose.

Smit with those charms, that must decay,
I grieve to see your future doom;
They died—nor were those flowers more gay,
The flowers that did in Eden bloom;
    Unpitying frosts, and Autumn's power
    Shall leave no vestige of this flower.

From morning suns and evening dews
At first thy little being came:
If nothing once, you nothing lose,
For when you die you are the same;
    The space between, is but an hour,
    The frail duration of a flower.

Song, for my Cat Suki : *Michael Connors*

I put my love in a cage of steel
Safer than houses
And more free;
I put my love in a steel cage
Whose bars were love's security.

He put my love in a cage of black,
Softer than metal
But less free;
He put my love in a black cage
Whose bars were death's reality.

I put my love in a cage of flame,
Quicker than silver
But less free;
I put my love in a gold cage
Whose bars were fire's purity.

We put our love in a cage of white,
Larger than living
And more free;
We put our love in a white cage
Whose bars are time's felicity.

Cages of steel and black and flame
In a white cage
Without a key;
My love lives free in the white cage
Of love's timeless serenity.

On Shooting a Swallow in Early Youth :
Charles Tennyson Turner

I hoard a little spring of secret tears,
For thee, poor bird; thy death-blow was my crime:
From the far past it has flow'd on for years;
It never dries; it brims at swallow-time.
No kindly voice within me took thy part,
Till I stood o'er thy last faint flutterings;
Since then, methinks, I have a gentler heart,
And gaze with pity all on wounded wings.
Full oft the vision of thy fallen head,
Twittering in highway dust, appeals to me;
Thy helpless form, as when I struck thee dead,
Drops out from every swallow-flight I see.
I would not have thine airy spirit laid,
I seem to love the little ghost I made.

Afters

Song : *John Keats*

I had a dove and the sweet dove died;
    And I have thought it died of grieving:
O, what could it grieve for? Its feet were tied,
    With a silken thread of my own hand's weaving;
Sweet little red feet! why should you die —
Why should you leave me, sweet bird! why?
You liv'd alone in the forest-tree,
Why, pretty thing! would you not live with me?
I kiss'd you oft and gave you white peas;
Why not live sweetly, as in the green trees?

Written for his lost Nightingale : *Alcuin*

Whoever stole you from that bush of broom,
    I think he envied me my happiness,
O little nightingale, for many a time
    You lightened my sad heart from its distress,
    And flooded my whole soul with melody.
And I would have the other birds all come,
    And sing along with me thy threnody.

So brown and dim that little body was,
    But none could scorn thy singing. In that throat
That tiny throat, what depth of harmony,
    And all night long ringing thy changing note.
    What marvel if the cherubim in heaven
Continually do praise Him, when to thee,
    O small and happy, such a grace was given?

(Translated from the Latin by Helen Waddell)

The Caged Goldfinch : *Thomas Hardy*

Within a churchyard, on a recent grave,
    I saw a little cage
That jailed a goldfinch. All was silence save
    Its hops from stage to stage.

There was inquiry in its wistful eye,
    And once it tried to sing;
Of him or her who placed it there, and why,
    No one knew anything.

Lady Lost : *John Crowe Ransom*

This morning flew up the lane
A timid lady bird to our birdbath
And eyed her image dolefully as death;
This afternoon, knocked on our windowpane
To be let in from the rain.

And when I caught her eye
She looked aside, but at the clapping thunder
And sight of the whole world blazing up like tinder
Looked in on us again most miserably,
Indeed as if she would cry.

So I will go out into the park and say,
"Who has lost a delicate brown-eyed lady
In the West End section? Or has anybody
Injured some fine woman in some dark way
Last night, or yesterday?

Let the owner come and claim possession,
No questions will be asked. But stroke her gently
With loving words, and she will evidently
Return to her full soft-haired white-breasted fashion
And her right home and her right passion."

To the Cuckoo : *William Wordsworth*

O blithe New-comer! I have heard,
I hear thee and rejoice.
O Cuckoo! shall I call thee Bird,
Or but a wandering Voice?

While I am lying on the grass
Thy twofold shout I hear;
From hill to hill it seems to pass
At once far off, and near.

Though babbling only to the Vale
Of sunshine and of flowers,
Thou bringest unto me a tale
Of visionary hours.

Afters

Thrice welcome, darling of the Spring!
Even yet thou art to me
No bird, but an invisible thing,
A voice, a mystery;

The same whom in my school-boy days
I listened to; that Cry
Which made me look a thousand ways
In bush, and tree, and sky.

To seek thee did I often rove
Through woods and on the green;
And thou wert still a hope, a love;
Still longed for, never seen.

And I can listen to thee yet;
Can lie upon the plain
And listen, till I do beget
That golden time again.

O blessèd Bird! the earth we pace
Again appears to be
An unsubstantial, faery place;
That is fit home for Thee!

Rachel at Kittyhawk : *Edward Brash*

Thinking of powered flight, Rachel races
nearly to the summit before she turns around and
waits for the remaining members of her vacationing
family. She is always first to reach a
destination: breathless, headlong, proud to
be the one we must catch up with. Here she animates
the hilltop with more of the Wrights' own
nerve than all the exhibitions in the world. Their
heavier-than-air craft made history that
day, its elegant design upheld by a combustion
engine; so Rachel, at the dawn of her age, flings
herself into the teeth of heaven only knows what
gales, her clothes pinned and the helmet
of her hair unbuckled by the wind.

Walking on Air : *Phoebe Hesketh*

To see her walking down the street
Demurely, with her flying feet
Folded like birds in buckskin neat,
To watch her wait all willow-grey
Against the wind, within the sway
Of Quaker skirts, who'd guess a gay
Green leprechaun slept deep in her?
For she can dance in dreams, and stir
Plain city men to weep for her.

The street is drab, yet pennons fly
The way she goes, and when we try
To walk with her she walks the sky.

Song for a Season : *Jeremy Robson*

Under a sun, under a moon
walk fast, walk slow,
and still the voices come
and still the voices go.

Rivers to the ocean
lovers to the war,
and still the waters freeze
and still the bombers soar.

Once I chased a shadow
once I stalked a ghost,
caught the voices lying
found I was their host.

And still the voices drum
and still the voices grow,
soldiers to the killing
driftwood to the flow.

Afters

The Legs : *Robert Graves*

There was this road,
And it led up-hill,
And it led down-hill,
And round and in and out.

And the traffic was legs,
Legs from the knees down,
Coming and going,
Never pausing.

And the gutters gurgled
With the rain's overflow,
And the sticks on the pavement
Blindly tapped and tapped.

What drew the legs along
Was the never-stopping,
And the senseless, frightening
Fate of being legs.

Legs for the road,
The road for legs,
Resolutely nowhere
In both directions.

My legs at least
Were not in that rout:
On grass by the roadside
Entire I stood,

Watching the unstoppable
Legs go by
With never a stumble
Between step and step.

Though my smile was broad
The legs could not see,
Though my laugh was loud
The legs could not hear.

My head dizzied, then:
I wondered suddenly,
Might I too be a walker
From the knees down?

Gently I touched my shins.
The doubt unchained them:
They had run in twenty puddles
Before I regained them.

Walking Song : Ivor Gurney

The miles go sliding by
Under my steady feet,
That mark a leisurely
And still unbroken beat,
Through coppices that hear
Awhile, then lie as still
As though no traveller
Ever had climbed their hill.

My comrades are the small
Or dumb or singing birds,
Squirrels, field-things all
And placid drowsing herds.
Companions that I must
Greet for a while, then leave
Scattering the forward dust
From dawn to late of eve.

Feet : *John Smith*

Listen, listen
There's walking in the world
All those feet
Your feet and mine;

Listen to the child's feet
Brushing on sand
Running on pebbles

They were once our feet
Your feet and mine

Listen to the quick feet
Dancing on wood
Heels tapping his feet
Toes tapping her feet

Afters

They were once our feet
Your feet and mine

Walking and running feet
Thumping and slurring feet
Light feet and heavy feet
Your feet, mine;

Keep the feet moving
Quick feet and slow feet
Your feet and my feet
Don't let them stop

Keep the feet moving
Your feet and my feet
Don't let them
Don't let them

The Soldier : *Rupert Brooke*

If I should die, think only this of me:
    That there's some corner of a foreign field
That is for ever England. There shall be
    In that rich earth a richer dust concealed;
A dust whom England bore, shaped, made aware,
    Gave, once, her flowers to love, her ways to roam;
A body of England's breathing English air,
    Washed by the rivers, blest by suns of home.

And think, this heart, all evil shed away,
    A pulse in the eternal mind, no less
        Gives somewhere back the thoughts by England given;
Her sights and sounds; dreams happy as her day;
    And laughter, learnt of friends; and gentleness,
        In hearts at peace, under an English heaven.

The Balance of Europe : *Alexander Pope*

Now Europe's balanced, neither Side prevails,
For nothing's left in either of the scales.

Heredity : *Thomas Hardy*

I am the family face;
Flesh perishes, I live on,
Projecting trait and trace
Through time to times anon,
And leaping from place to place
Over oblivion.

The years-heired feature that can
In curve and voice and eye
Despise the human span
Of durance—that is I;
The eternal thing in man,
That heeds no call to die.

Man : *William Browne*

Like to a silkworm of one year,
Or like a wronged lover's tear,
Or on the waves a rudder's dint,
Or like the sparkles of a flint,
Or like to little cakes perfum'd,
Or fireworks made to be consumed;
Even such is man, and all that trust
In weak and animated dust.
The silkworm droops; the tear's soon shed;
The ship's way lost; the sparkle dead;
The cake is burnt; the firework done;
And man as these as quickly gone.

Full Fathom Five : *William Shakespeare*

Full fathom five thy father lies;
    Of his bones are coral made;
Those are pearls that were his eyes:
    Nothing of him that doth fade,
But doth suffer a sea-change
Into something rich and strange.
Sea-nymphs hourly ring his knell:
                Ding-dong.
Hark! now I hear them—Ding-dong, bell.

Afters

Even Such is Time : *Walter Raleigh*

Even such is Time, that takes in trust
Our youth, our joys, our all we have,
And pays us but with earth and dust;
Who in the dark and silent grave,
When we have wandered all our ways,
Shuts up the story of our days.
But from this earth, this grave, this dust,
My God shall raise me up, I trust.

Epitaph : *Herbert Read*

Yes yes
and ever it will come to this:
Life folds like a fan with a click!
The hand that lately beat the air
with an arch of painted silk
falls listless in the lap.

The air
the agitation and the flush
close and collapse. A rigid frame
restricts the limbs that once ran free
across the hearth across the fields
over the threatening hills.

Farewell : *Walter de la Mare*

When I lie where shades of darkness
Shall no more assail mine eyes,
Nor the rain make lamentation
    When the wind sighs;
How will fare the world whose wonder
Was the very proof of me?
Memory fades, must the remembered
    Perishing be?

Oh, when this my dust surrenders
Hand, foot, lip, to dust again,
May these loved and loving faces
    Please other men!

May the rusting harvest hedgerow
Still the Traveller's Joy entwine,
And as happy children gather
    Posies once mine.

Look thy last on all things lovely,
Every hour. Let no night
Seal thy sense in deathly slumber
    Till to delight
Thou have paid thy utmost blessing;
Since that all things thou would'st praise
Beauty took from those who loved them
    In other days.

Song : *Christina Rossetti*

When I am dead, my dearest,
    Sing no sad songs for me;
Plant thou no roses at my head,
    Nor shady cypress tree:
Be the green grass above me
    With showers and dewdrops wet;
And if thou wilt, remember
    And if thou wilt, forget.

I shall not see the shadows,
    I shall not feel the rain;
I shall not hear the nightingale
    Sing on as if in pain;
And dreaming through the twilight
    That doth not rise nor set,
Haply I may remember,
    And haply may forget.

Salt and Pepper : *Samuel Menashe*

Here and there
White hairs appear
On my chest—
Age seasons me
Gives me zest—
I am a sage
In the making
Sprinkled, shaking

Afters

Afterwards : *Thomas Hardy*

When the Present has latched its postern behind my tremulous stay,
    And the May month flaps its glad green leaves like wings,
Delicate-filmed as new-spun silk, will the neighbours say,
    "He was a man who used to notice such things"?

If it be in the dusk when, like an eyelid's soundless blink,
    The dewfall-hawk comes crossing the shades to alight
Upon the wind-warped upland thorn, a gazer may think,
    "To him this must have been a familiar sight."

If I pass during some nocturnal blackness, mothy and warm,
    When the hedgehog travels furtively over the lawn,
One may say, "He strove that such innocent creatures should come
                                                            to no harm
But he could do little for them; and now he is gone."

If, when hearing that I have been stilled at last, they stand at the
                                                            door,
    Watching the full-starred heavens that winter sees,
Will this thought rise on those who will meet my face no more,
    "He was one who had an eye for such mysteries"?

And will any say when my bell of quittance is heard in the gloom,
    And a crossing breeze cuts a pause in its outrollings,
Till they rise again, as they were a new bell's boom,
    "He hears it not now, but used to notice such things"?

The Passing Cloud : *Stevie Smith*

From the Royal Bethlehem Hospital

I thought as I lay on my bed one night, I am only a passing Cloud
And I wiped the tear from my sorrowful eye and merrily cried aloud
Oh the love of the Lord is a fearful thing and the love of the Lord is
                                                            mine

And what do I care for the sins of men and the tears of our guilty
                                                                    time
I will sail my cloud in the bright blue sky, in the bright blue sky I sail
And I look at the sea so merrily swung in the path of the Arctic whale
On the tropic belt of the uttermost wild the sea rings a merry peal
And the fish leaps up and the sharks pursue in Creation's happy reel
Oh I dance on my cloud and I cry aloud to the careless creative gust
That made us all and made the fish and the ocean that holds them fast
Hurrah hurrah for the grand old heavenly gusty creator Lord
Who said to Job, Don't bother me son, I'll do as I please my word.
Oh never was happiness like to mine as I pelt along on my cloud
In the sky-blue path of the high winds' breath, no wonder I cry aloud
With joy I cried and my cheeks were wet and the air was a singing
                                                                    space
And I thought as we shot to the upper reach, My lord, it's a lick of a
                                                                    pace.
When we swept out of sight of the troublesome earth, was I afraid,
                                                                    oh no,
I was glad to see the parochial thing pack up its traps and go
And now I go round and round I go in the merry abyss of the sky
Piercing the grand primæval dust of the stars in their infancy
I tunnel, I burrow, I offer my dust as a dust for creation's choice
And in the ding-dong of the universe I pipe my innocent voice
I pipe my innocent voice I pipe, I pipe and I also sing
Till I'd sung too loud and woke myself up and that is another thing,

Oh I woke with a bump and they brought me here to Bethlehem's
                                                        Royal precincts
And do I care? Not I, not I, I have shed all careful instincts,
I will laugh and sing, or be dumb if they please, and await at the
                                                        Lord's discretion
The day I'll be one, as one I'll be, in an infinite regression
One, ha ha, with a merry ha ha, skip the fish and amoeba where are
                                                                    we now?
We are very far out, in a rarified place, with the thin thin dust in a
                                                                    giddy chase,
The dust of Continuous Creation, and how is that for identification?
You'll like it; you must, you know,
That merry dust does jig so.

Index of first lines

INDEX OF FIRST LINES

INDEX OF FIRST LINES

Index of Authors

INDEX OF AUTHORS